Kaplan Publish[ing]
ways to make [...]
exciting online [...]
different to stu[...]

This book come[s...]
that you can stu[...]

Having purchased this book, you ha[...]

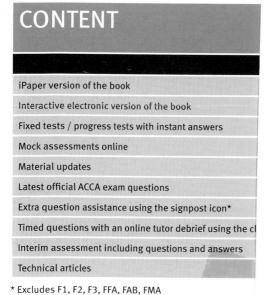

CONTENT

iPaper version of the book
Interactive electronic version of the book
Fixed tests / progress tests with instant answers
Mock assessments online
Material updates
Latest official ACCA exam questions
Extra question assistance using the signpost icon*
Timed questions with an online tutor debrief using the c[...]
Interim assessment including questions and answers
Technical articles

* Excludes F1, F2, F3, FFA, FAB, FMA

How to access your online resource[s]

Kaplan Financial students will already have a Kaplan EN-gage account and these extra resources will be available to you online. You do not need to register again, as this process was completed when you enrolled. If you are having problems accessing online materials, please ask your course administrator.

If you are already a registered Kaplan EN-gage user go to www.EN-gage.co.uk and log in. Select the 'add a book' feature and enter the ISBN number of this book and the unique pass key at the bottom of this card. Then click 'finished' or 'add another book'. You may add as many books as you have purchased from this screen.

If you purchased through Kaplan Flexible Learning or via the Kaplan Publishing website you will automatically receive an e-mail invitation to Kaplan EN·gage online. Please register your details using this email to gain access to your content. If you do not receive the e-mail or book content, please contact Kaplan Flexible Learning.

If you are a new Kaplan EN-gage user register at www.EN-gage.co.uk and click on the link contained in the email we sent you to activate your account. Then select the 'add a book' feature, enter the ISBN number of this book and the unique pass key at the bottom of this card. Then click 'finished' or 'add another book'.

Your Code and Information

This code can only be used once for the registration of one book online. This registration and your online content will expire when the final sittings for the examinations covered by this book have taken place. Please allow one hour from the time you submit your book details for us to process your request.

Please scratch the film to access your EN-gage code.

Please be aware that this code is case-sensitive and you will need to include the dashes within the passcode, but not when entering the ISBN. For further technical support, please visit www.EN-gage.co.uk

 KAPLAN PUBLISHING

Professional Examinations

Level 3

Costs and Revenues

REVISION KIT

British Library Cataloguing-in-Publication Data

A catalogue record for this book is available from the British Library.

Published by:

Kaplan Publishing UK

Unit 2 The Business Centre

Molly Millar's Lane

Wokingham

Berkshire

RG41 2QZ

ISBN: 978-0-85732-622-5

© Kaplan Financial Limited, 2012

Printed and bound in Great Britain

CONTENTS

Features in this revision kit

In addition to providing a wide ranging bank of real exam style questions, we have also included in this kit:

- Paper specific information and advice on exam technique.

- Our recommended approach to make your revision for this particular subject as effective as possible.

You will find a wealth of other resources to help you with your studies on the AAT website:

www.aat.org.uk/

INDEX TO QUESTIONS AND ANSW[cut off]

EXAM TECHNIQUE

- **Do not skip any of the material** in the syllabus.

- **Read each question** *very* carefully.

- **Double-check your answer** before committing yourself to it.

- Answer **every** question – if you do not know an answer to a multiple choice question or true/false question, you don't lose anything by guessing. Think carefully before you **guess**.

- If you are answering a multiple-choice question, **eliminate first those answers that you know are wrong**. Then choose the most appropriate answer from those that are left.

- **Don't panic** if you realise you've answered a question incorrectly. Getting one question wrong will not mean the difference between passing and failing

Computer-based exams – tips

- Do not attempt a CBA until you have **completed all study material** relating to it.

- On the AAT website there is a CBA demonstration. It is **ESSENTIAL** that you attempt this before your real CBA. You will become familiar with how to move around the CBA screens and the way that questions are formatted, increasing your confidence and speed in the actual exam.

- Be sure you understand how to use the **software** before you start the exam. If in doubt, ask the assessment centre staff to explain it to you.

- Questions are **displayed on the screen** and answers are entered using keyboard and mouse. At the end of the exam, you are given a certificate showing the result you have achieved.

- In addition to the traditional multiple-choice question type, CBAs will also contain **other types of questions**, such as number entry questions, drag and drop, true/false, pick lists or drop down menus or hybrids of these.

- You need to be sure you **know how to answer questions** of this type before you sit the exam, through practice.

PAPER SPECIFIC INFORMATION

THE EXAM

FORMAT OF THE ASSESSMENT

The exam is divided into two sections:

Section 1 is concerned with the knowledge and techniques required for dealing with direct costs and revenues, and with the treatment of overhead costs in the short term. This includes calculation and/or explanations relating to inventory control, cost accounting journals, direct labour cost, allocation and apportionment of indirect costs to responsibility centres and overhead absorption rates including under and over absorptions.

Section 2 is concerned with the knowledge and techniques required for decision-making, using both short term and long term estimates of costs and revenues. This includes calculations and/or explanations relating to changes in unit costs/profit as activity levels change and profit/loss by product, break-even (CVP) analysis, limiting factor decision making, process costing, reconciling budget and actual costs and revenues by means of flexible or fixed budgets and capital investment appraisal

Learning objectives

On completion of these units the learner will be able to:

- demonstrate an understanding of the role of costing within the organisation

- advise on the most appropriate costing methods to use within an organisation

- understand the principles of using costing as a decision making tool

- record and analyse information relating to costs

- apportion costs according to organisational requirements

- correctly identify any significant deviations and report these to management

Time allowed

2 ½ hours

PASS MARK

The pass mark for all AAT CBAs is 70%.

 Always keep your eye on the clock and make sure you attempt all questions!

DETAILED SYLLABUS

The detailed syllabus and study guide written by the AAT can be found at:

www.aat.org.uk/

KAPLAN'S RECOMMENDED REVISION APPROACH

QUESTION PRACTICE IS THE KEY TO SUCCESS

Success in professional examinations relies upon you acquiring a firm grasp of the required knowledge at the tuition phase. In order to be able to do the questions, knowledge is essential.

However, the difference between success and failure often hinges on your exam technique on the day and making the most of the revision phase of your studies.

The **Kaplan textbook** is the starting point, designed to provide the underpinning knowledge to tackle all questions. However, in the revision phase, poring over text books is not the answer.

The Kaplan workbook helps you consolidate your knowledge and understanding and is a useful tool to check whether you can remember key topic areas.

Kaplan pocket notes are designed to help you quickly revise a topic area, however you then need to practise questions. There is a need to progress to exam style questions as soon as possible, and to tie your exam technique and technical knowledge together.

The importance of question practice cannot be over-emphasised.

The recommended approach below is designed by expert tutors in the field, in conjunction with their knowledge of the examiner and the specimen assessment.

You need to practise as many questions as possible in the time you have left.

OUR AIM

Our aim is to get you to the stage where you can attempt exam questions confidently, to time, in a closed book environment, with no supplementary help (i.e. to simulate the real examination experience).

Practising your exam technique is also vitally important for you to assess your progress and identify areas of weakness that may need more attention in the final run up to the examination.

In order to achieve this we recognise that initially you may feel the need to practice some questions with open book help.

Good exam technique is vital.

THE KAPLAN CRS REVISION PLAN

Stage 1: Assess areas of strengths and weaknesses

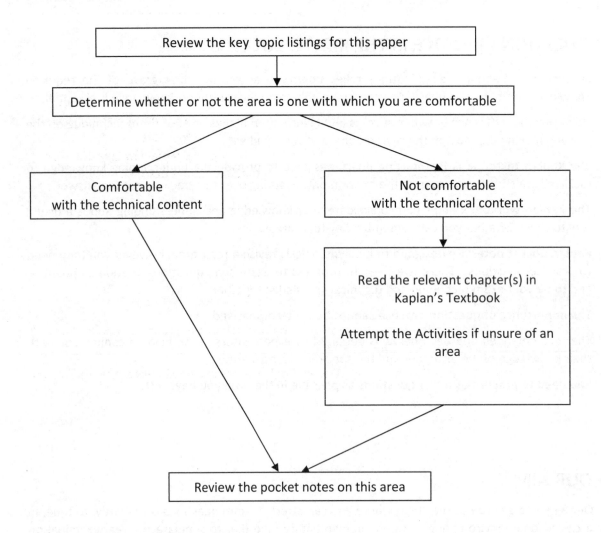

Review the key topic listings for this paper

Determine whether or not the area is one with which you are comfortable

Comfortable
with the technical content

Not comfortable
with the technical content

Read the relevant chapter(s) in
Kaplan's Textbook

Attempt the Activities if unsure of an
area

Review the pocket notes on this area

Stage 2: Practise questions

Follow the order of revision of topics as presented in this kit and attempt the questions in the order suggested.

Try to avoid referring to text books and notes and the model answer until you have completed your attempt.

Review your attempt with the model answer and assess how much of the answer you achieved.

Stage 3: Final pre-exam revision

We recommend that you **attempt at least one two hour mock examination** containing a set of previously unseen exam standard questions.

Attempt the mock CBA online in timed, closed book conditions to simulate the real exam experience

Section 1

PRACTICE QUESTIONS

PRINCIPLES OF COST ACCOUNTING

COST BEHAVIOURS

1   The following data relate to two output levels of a department:

Machine hours	17,000	18,500
Overheads	£246,500	£251,750

The amount of fixed overheads is:

A   £5,250

B   £59,500

C   £187,000

D   £246,500

2   A manufacturing company has four types of cost (identified as T1, T2, T3 and T4).

The total cost for each type at two different production levels is:

Cost type	Total cost for 125 units £	Total cost for 180 units £
T1	1,000	1,260
T2	1,750	2,520
T3	2,475	2,826
T4	3,225	4,644

Which two cost types would be classified as being semi-variable?

A   T1 and T3

B   T1 and T4

C   T2 and T3

D   T2 and T4

3 **Identify the TWO types of cost behaviour shown below:**

Graph 1   **Graph 2**

Total cost £   Total cost £

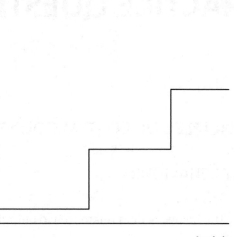

Activity   Activity

A	Variable	A	Variable
B	Fixed	B	Fixed
C	Semi variable	C	Semi variable
D	Stepped fixed	D	Stepped fixed

4 **Fill in the blanks using the words listed below:**

_____ costs are ones that can be economically and exclusively identified with a cost unit. Examples include _____ used in production of clothing and _____ used in the manufacture of computers.

_____ costs, or _____ , are costs that cannot be economically and exclusively identified with a cost unit. Examples include _____.

Direct
Indirect
Fabric
Light, heat and power costs
Electrical components
Overheads

5   Cartcyle Ltd has prepared a forecast for the next quarter for one of its wooden products, DR43. This component is produced in batches and the forecast is based on selling and producing 2,160 batches.

One of the customers of Cartcyle Ltd has indicated that it may be significantly increasing its order level for product DR43 for the next quarter and it appears that activity levels of 2,700 batches and 3,600 batches are feasible.

The semi-variable costs should be calculated using the high-low method. If 5,400 batches are sold the total semi-variable cost will be £13,284, and there is a constant unit variable cost up to this volume.

Complete the table below and calculate the estimated profit per batch of DR43 at the different activity levels.

Batches produced and sold	2,160	2,700	3,600
	£	£	£
Sales revenue	64,800		
Variable costs:			
• Direct materials	9,720		
• Direct labour	22,680		
• Overheads	12,960		
Semi-variable costs:	6,804		
• Variable element			
• Fixed element			
Total cost	52,164		
Total profit	12,636		
Profit per batch (to 2 decimal places)	5.85		

6 Charter Flights profit centre has just revised its forecasts for the number of miles it expects to fly during the next month on a particular charter contract. Originally it expected the contract would be for flights totalling 5,000 miles. Charter Flights now expects that the total miles to be flown will increase to either 6,000 or 7,000 miles.

Notes:
- The company chartering the flights has negotiated with Charter Flights a reduction of 10% per mile, paid on all miles flown in excess of the 5,000 miles agreed in the original contract.
- Landing and servicing fees are a semi-variable cost. There is a fixed charge of £600,000 plus £50/mile.

Complete the table below and calculate the estimated profit per batch of DR43 at the different activity levels.

Likely miles	5,000	6,000	7,000
	£000	£000	£000
Sale revenue	2,500		
Variable/semi-variable costs:			
• Aviation fuel	400		
• Landing and servicing fees	850		
• Other variable overheads	135		
Fixed costs:			
• Wages and salaries	420		
• Other fixed overheads	625		
Total cost	2430		
Total profit	70		
Profit per mile flown (2 decimal places) £	14.00		

7   Grape Ltd has prepared a forecast for the next quarter for one of its statues – Owl. Owl is produced in batches and the forecast is based on selling and producing 800 batches.

One of the customers of Grape Ltd has indicated that it may be significantly increasing its order level for Owl for the next quarter and it appears that activity levels of 1,200 batches and 1,500 batches are feasible.

The semi-variable costs should be calculated using the high-low method. If 1,600 batches are sold the total semi-variable cost will be £4,920, and there is a constant unit variable cost up to this volume.

Complete the table below and calculate the estimated profit per batch of Owl at the different activity levels.

Batches produced and sold	800	1,200	1,500
	£	£	£
Sales revenue	24,000		
Variable costs:			
• Direct materials	3,600		
• Direct labour	8,400		
• Overheads	1,800		
Semi-variable costs:	2,520		
• Variable element			
• Fixed element			
Total cost	16,320		
Total profit	7,680		
Profit per batch (to 2 decimal places)	9.60		

MATERIAL COSTS

INVENTORY RECORDS

8   **PLASTIC**

The following information is available for plastic grade PM7:

- Annual demand 112,500 kilograms.
- Annual holding cost per kilogram £1.80
- Fixed ordering cost £3.60

(a)   **Calculate the Economic Order Quantity (EOQ) for PM7 (round to the nearest whole number)**

The inventory record shown below for plastic grade PM7 for the month of July has only been fully completed for the first three weeks of the month.

(b)   **Complete the entries in the inventory record for the two receipts on 24 and 28 July that were ordered using the EOQ method.**

(c)   **Complete ALL entries in the inventory record for the two issues in the month and for the closing balance at the end of July using the FIFO method of issuing inventory.**

(Show the costs per kilogram (kg) in £'s to 3 decimal places; and the total costs in whole £'s).

Inventory record for plastic grade PM7

Date	Receipts Quantity kgs	Cost per kg (£)	Total cost (£)	Issues Quantity kgs	Cost per kg (£)	Total cost (£)	Balance Quantity kgs	Total cost (£)
Balance as at 22 July							198	238
24 July		2.336						
26 July				540				
28 July		2.344						
30 July				710				

9 SURESTICK GLUE

The following information is available for direct material SURESTICK GLUE:

- Fixed ordering cost £2.50
- Annual holding cost per litre £1.00
- Monthly demand 2,500 litres

(a) **Calculate the Economic Order Quantity (EOQ) for direct material SURESTICK GLUE (round your answer up to the nearest whole number)**

The inventory record shown below for SURESTICK GLUE for the month of June has only been fully completed for the first three weeks of the month.

(b) **Complete the entries in the inventory record for the two receipts on 24 and 27 June that were ordered using the EOQ method.**

(c) **Complete ALL entries in the inventory record for the two issues in the month and for the closing balance at the end of June using the AVCO method of issuing inventory.**

(Show the costs per litre in £'s to 3 decimal places; and the total costs in whole £'s, round up to nearest whole number).

Inventory record for SURESTICK GLUE

Date	Receipts			Issues			Balance	
	Quantity litres	Cost per litre (£)	Total cost (£)	Quantity litres	Cost per litre (£)	Total cost (£)	Quantity Litres	Total cost (£)
Balance as at 23 June							65	130
24 June		2.234						
26 June				180				
27 June		2.341						
30 June				250				

10 GRAPE LTD

The inventory record shown below for glaze for the month of January has only been fully completed for the first three weeks of the month.

(a) **Identify the inventory valuation method used to complete the inventory record:**

    A   FIFO

    B   LIFO

    C   AVCO

(b) **Complete ALL entries in the inventory record for the two issues in the month and for the closing balance at the end of January using the method of issuing inventory identified in part (a)**

(Show the costs per drum in £'s to 3 decimal places; and the total costs in whole £'s).

Inventory record for glaze

Date	Receipts			Issues			Balance	
	Quantity drums	Cost per drum (£)	Total cost (£)	Quantity drums	Cost per drum (£)	Total cost (£)	Quantity drums	Total cost (£)
Balance as at 22 January							1,650	1,980
25 January	1,200	1.250					2,850	3,480
26 January				1,300		1,587		
28 January	1,200	1.302						
31 January				1,500				

11 GLOBE LTD

(a) Identify the inventory valuation method used to complete the inventory record:

A   FIFO

B   LIFO

C   AVCO

(b) Complete ALL entries in the inventory record for the two issues in the month and for the closing balance at the end of March using the method of issuing inventory identified in part (a).

(Show the costs per tonne in £'s to 2 decimal places; and the total costs in whole £'s).

Inventory record for M2

Date	Receipts Quantity tonnes	Receipts Cost per tonne (£)	Receipts Total cost (£)	Issues Quantity tonnes	Issues Cost per tonne (£)	Issues Total cost (£)	Balance Quantity tonnes	Balance Total cost (£)
Balance as at 27 March							1,200	14,400
28 March	800	12.50					2,000	24,400
29 March				820		9,840		
30 March	800	12.25						
31 March				900				

12 In a period of rising prices, which type of inventory valuation shows the highest profit?

A   FIFO

B   LIFO

C   AVCO

D   None

13 In times of rising prices, the valuation of inventory using the First In First Out method, as opposed to the Weighted Average Cost method, will result in which ONE of the following combinations?

	Cost of sales	Profit	Closing inventory
A	Lower	Higher	Higher
B	Lower	Higher	Lower
C	Higher	Lower	Higher
D	Higher	Higher	Lower

MATERIAL BOOKKEEPING

14   The following represent the materials transactions for a company for the month of December 20X6:

	£000s
Materials purchases	176
Issued to production	165
Materials written off	4
Returned to stores	9
Returned to suppliers	8

The material inventory at 1 December 20X6 was £15,000.

What is the closing balance on the materials inventory account at 31 December 20X6?

A   £5,000

B   £16,000

C   £23,000

D   £31,000

15   **Put the correct entries into the Journal below to record the following FOUR accounting transactions:**

1   Receipt of SURESTICK GLUE into inventory paying immediately by BACS.

2   Issue of SURESTICK GLUE from inventory to production.

3   Receipt of SURESTICK GLUE into inventory paying on credit.

4   Return of SURESTICK GLUE from production to inventory.

The choices are:

A   Dr. Bank, Cr. Inventory

B   Dr. Trade Payables' Control, Cr. Inventory

C   Dr. Inventory, Cr. Bank

D   Dr. Inventory, Cr. Trade Payables' Control

E   Dr. Inventory, Cr. Production

F   Dr. Production, Cr. Inventory

	Choice
Transaction 1	
Transaction 2	
Transaction 3	
Transaction 4	

16 **Put the correct entries into the Journal below to record the following FOUR accounting transactions:**

1   Receipt of glaze into inventory paying on credit.

2   Write off of glaze.

3   Receipt of glaze into inventory paying immediately by BACS.

4   Return of glaze to the supplier.

The choices are:

A   Dr. Bank, Cr. Inventory

B   Dr. Trade Payables' Control, Cr. Inventory

C   Dr. Inventory, Cr. Bank

D   Dr. Inventory, Cr. Trade Payables' Control

E   Dr. Inventory, Cr. Production

F   Dr. Income statement, Cr. Inventory

	Choice
Transaction 1	
Transaction 2	
Transaction 3	
Transaction 4	

17 **The double entry for an issue of indirect production materials would be:**

A	Dr Materials control account	Cr Finished goods control account
B	Dr Production overhead control a/c	Cr Materials control account
C	Dr Work-in-progress control account	Cr Production overhead control a/c
D	Dr Work-in-progress control account	Cr Materials control account

LABOUR COSTS

18   CARTCYLE LTD

Below is a weekly timesheet for one of Cartcyle Ltd's employees, who is paid as follows:

- For a basic six-hour shift every day from Monday to Friday – basic pay.
- For any overtime in excess of the basic six hours, on any day from Monday to Friday – the extra hours are paid at time-and-a-half (basic pay plus an overtime premium equal to half of basic pay).
- For three contracted hours each Saturday morning – basic pay.
- For any hours in excess of three hours on Saturday – the extra hours are paid at double time (basic pay plus an overtime premium equal to basic pay).
- For any hours worked on Sunday – paid at double time (basic pay plus an overtime premium equal to basic pay).

Complete the columns headed Basic pay, Overtime premium and Total pay:

(**Notes:** Zero figures should be entered in cells where appropriate)

Employee's weekly timesheet for week ending 7 December

Employee: A.Man			Profit Centre: Wood finishing			
Employee number: C812			Basic pay per hour: £8.00			
	Hours spent on production	Hours worked on indirect work	Notes	Basic pay £	Overtime premium £	Total pay £
Monday	6	2	10am–12am cleaning of machinery			
Tuesday	2	4	9am–1pm customer care course			
Wednesday	8					
Thursday	6					
Friday	6	1	3–4pm health and safety training			
Saturday	6					
Sunday	3					
Total	**37**	**7**				

19 A company employs a group of production workers who, as well as earning basic pay, are also paid a weekly group bonus based on their productivity during each week.

The group has a standard (target) output of 800 units of production per hour worked. All output in excess of this level earns a bonus for each of the employees.

The bonus % is calculated as:

25% × $\dfrac{\text{Excess production (units)}}{\text{Standard production (units)}}$ × 100

The bonus rate per hour is then calculated as: bonus % x £10.

The following information relates to this group's performance last week:

	Hours worked	Actual production (units)
Monday	920	940,000
Tuesday	870	890,000
Wednesday	910	930,000
Thursday	920	960,000
Friday	940	990,000
Saturday	440	690,000
Total	5,000	5,400,000

(a) **Use the table below to calculate the group bonus rate per hour and the total bonus to be paid to the group.**

	Units
Actual production	
Less standard production (based on actual hours worked)	
Excess production	
Bonus %	
Group bonus rate per hour £	
Total group bonus £	

(b) **An employee in this group worked for 44 hours last week, and is paid a basic rate of £9.60 per hour. The employee's total pay for last week was:**

£   .

20   GRAPES

Below is a weekly timesheet for one of Grape's employees, who is paid as follows:

- For a basic seven-hour shift every day from Monday to Friday – basic pay.
- For any overtime in excess of the basic seven hours, on any day from Monday to Friday – the extra hours are paid at basic pay. An overtime premium is added of 50% of basic time.
- For two contracted hours each Saturday morning – basic pay.
- For any hours in excess of two hours on Saturday – the overtime premium is paid at 75% of basic pay.

Complete the columns headed Basic pay, Overtime premium and Total pay:

(**Notes:** Zero figures should be entered in cells where appropriate)

Employee's weekly timesheet for week ending 31 January

Employee: Olivia Michael			**Profit Centre:** Moulding Department			
Employee number: P450			**Basic pay per hour:** £10.00			
	Hours spent in work	*Hours spent on indirect work*	*Notes*	*Basic pay* £	*Overtime premium* £	*Total pay* £
Monday	8	3	10am–1pm cleaning moulds			
Tuesday	7	4	9am–1pm fire training			
Wednesday	8					
Thursday	7	1				
Friday	7	1	3–4pm annual appraisal			
Saturday	3					
Total	**40**	**9**				

Analysis the timesheet into production and production overhead costs

Labour cost account

	£		£
Bank		Production	
		Production Overheads	

21 The payroll for maintenance employees for the week ending 30 November has been completed. The following payments are to be made:

	£
Net wages/salaries to pay to employees	10,000
Income tax and national insurance contributions (NIC) to pay to HMRC	2,000
Pension contributions to pay to F4L pension scheme	1,000
Gross payroll costs	13,000

The payroll for the week is analysed as:

	£
Direct labour costs	7,000
Indirect labour costs	4,000
Maintenance administration labour costs	2,000
Gross payroll costs	13,000

The following cost account codes are used to record maintenance labour costs:

Code	Description
6200	Maintenance direct labour
6400	Maintenance overheads
6600	Maintenance administration
8200	Wages control

(a) **Complete the wages control account entries in the account shown below:**

Wages control account			
	£		£
Bank (net wages/salaries)		Maintenance (direct labour)	
HMRC (income tax and NIC)		Maintenance overheads	
Pension contributions		Maintenance administration	
	13,000		13,000

(b)   Complete the table below to show how the gross payroll cost for the week is charged to the various cost accounts of the business:

Date	Code	Debit	Credit
30 November			
30 November			
30 November			
30 November			
30 November			
30 November			

22   Put the correct entries into the Journal below to record the following FOUR accounting transactions:

1   Record labour costs in the cost ledger

2   Analyse direct labour costs

3   Record indirect labour costs

4   Record additional production overheads

The choices are:

A   Dr. Wages control, Cr. Bank

B   Dr. Work-in-progress, Cr. Wages control

C   Dr. Production overhead account, Cr. Wages Control

D   Dr. Production overhead control, Cr. Bank

E   Dr. Inventory, Cr. Production

F   Dr. Production, Cr. Inventory

	Choice
Transaction 1	
Transaction 2	
Transaction 3	
Transaction 4	

23 The following information relates to direct labour costs incurred in producing 57,600 labelled soft drink bottles during May:

Normal time hours worked	900 hours
Overtime at time and a half worked	180 hours
Overtime at double time worked	135 hours
Total hours worked	1,215 hours
Normal time hourly rate	£8 per hour

Overtime premiums paid are included as part of direct labour cost.

A trainee accounts clerk has produced the following incorrect calculation of the total cost of direct labour used to produce these bottles:

	£
Cost at normal rate - 1,215 hours at £8 =	9,720
Cost at time and a half - 135 hours at £12 =	1,620
Cost at double time - 180 hours at £16=	2,880
Total direct labour cost	**14,220**

(a) **Calculate the correct total cost of direct labour used to produce the bottles during May.**

£ [   ]

(b) **Calculate the direct labour cost per soft drink bottle.**

£ [.   ]

24

A company operates a piecework system of remuneration. Employees must work for a minimum of 37 hours per week. Sebastian produces the following output for a particular week:

Product	Quantity	Standard time per item (hours)	Total actual time (hours)
Buckles	50	0.2	9
Press studs	200	0.06	14
Belts	100	0.1	12
Buttons	10	0.7	6
			41

Sebastian is paid £8.00 per standard hour worked. What are his earnings for the week?

A   £296

B   £302

C   £312

D   £328

ABSORPTION AND MARGINAL COSTING

25 **Which of the following are true of marginal costing?**

(i) The marginal cost of a product includes an allowance for fixed production costs.

(ii) The marginal cost of a product represents the additional cost of producing an extra unit.

(iii) If the inventory increases over a year, the profits under absorption costing will be lower than with marginal costing.

A (i) only

B (ii) only

C (ii) and (iii) only

D (i), (ii) and (iii)

26 **Which of these statements are true of marginal costing?**

(i) The contribution per unit will be constant if the sales volume increases.

(ii) There is no under- or over-absorption of overheads.

(iii) Marginal costing does not provide useful information for decision making.

A (i) and (ii) only

B (ii) and (iii) only

C (ii) only

D (i), (ii) and (iii)

27 **The following information relates to a contract for transporting school children during May 2007:**

	£
Fuel and other variable overheads	9,200
Fixed costs:	
Drivers' wages, pension and national insurance	3,220
Other fixed overheads	23,000
Number of miles travelled	4,600

Calculate the cost per mile under:

(a) **Marginal costing**

£ .

(b) **Absorption costing**

£ .

28   Globe Ltd has prepared a forecast for the next quarter for Tomato fertilizer.

Globe budgets to produce 1,800kg of the fertiliser and sell 1,000kg. The cost and revenue for this budget is as follows:

	£000
Sales	50,000
Direct materials	7,560
Direct labour	17,640
Fixed Production Overheads	3,600
Advertising (fixed cost)	2,010

Globe has no opening stock of the fertilizer.

Produce a marginal costing income statement and an absorption costing income statement

Marginal Costing	£000	£000
Sales		
Opening inventory		
Production costs		
Less: Closing inventory		
Less: Cost of sales		
Contribution		
Less: Fixed costs		
Profit for the period		

Absorption Costing	£000	£000
Sales		
Opening inventory		
Production costs		
Less: Closing inventory		
Lee: Cost of sales		
Gross Profit		
Less: Non-production cost		
Profit for the period		

Reconcile the two profits:

	£000
Absorption costing profit	
Marginal costing profit	

29 **ILCB has the following information relating to one of its products:**

- Selling price per unit   £12
- Prime cost per unit   £4
- Variable production cost per unit   £3
- Budgeted fixed production overhead   £30,000 per month
- Budgeted production   15,000 units
- Budgeted sales   12,000 units per month
- Opening inventory   2,000 units

Produce a marginal costing income statement and an absorption costing income statement

Marginal Costing	£	£
Sales		
Opening inventory		
Production costs		
Less: Closing inventory		
Less: Cost of sales		
Contribution		
Less: Fixed costs		
Profit for the period		

Absorption Costing	£	£
Sales		
Opening inventory		
Production costs		
Less: Closing inventory		
Less: Cost of sales		
Gross Profit		
Less: Non-production cost		
Profit for the period		

Reconcile the two profits:

	£
Absorption costing profit	
Marginal costing profit	

30 CPL is considering what the effect would be of costing its products under marginal costing principles, instead of under absorption costing principles that it currently follows.

The following information relates to one of the company's products:

- Selling price per unit   £40
- Prime cost per unit   £12
- Variable production overhead cost per unit   £4
- Budgeted fixed production overhead   £120,000 per month
- Budgeted production   12,000 units
- Budgeted sales   10,000 per month
- Opening inventory   500 units

(a) **Calculate the contribution per unit:**

£

(b) **Calculate the profit per unit:**

£

(c) **Complete the table below to produce an Income Statement for the product for the month under marginal costing principles.**

	£	£
Sales		
Opening inventory		
Variable production costs		
Less: Closing inventory		
Less: Cost of sales		
Contribution		
Less: Fixed costs		
Profit		

(d)   **Complete the table below to produce an Income Statement for the product for the month under absorption costing principles.**

	£	£
Sales		
Opening inventory		
Production costs		
Less: Closing inventory		
Less: Cost of sales		
Profit		

31   A new company has set up a marginal costing system and has a budgeted profit for the period of £23,000 based on sales of 13,000 units and production of 15,000 units. This level of production represents the firm's expected long-term level of production. The company's budgeted fixed production costs are £3,000 for the period.

If the company were to change to an absorption costing system the budgeted profit would be:

A   £22,600

B   £23,400

C   £25,600

D   £26,400

ACCOUNTING FOR OVERHEADS

OVERHEAD ALLOCATION AND APPORTIONMENT

32   What is cost apportionment?

A   The charging of discrete identifiable items of cost to cost centres or cost units

B   The collection of costs attributable to cost centres and cost units using the costing methods, principles and techniques prescribed for a particular business entity

C   The process of establishing the costs of cost centres or cost units

D   The division of costs amongst two or more cost centres in proportion to the estimated benefit received, using a proxy, e.g. square feet

33   Cartcyle Ltd

Cartcyle Ltd's budgeted overheads for the next financial year are:

	£	£
Depreciation of plant and equipment		1,447,470
Power for production machinery		1,287,000
Rent and rates		188,100
Light and heat		41,580
Indirect labour costs:		
Maintenance	182,070	
Stores	64,890	
Administration	432,180	
Total indirect labour cost		679,140

The following information is also available:

Department	Net book value of plant and equipment.	Production machinery power usage (KwH)	Floor space (square metres)	Number of employees
Production:				
Wood cutting	10,080,000	3,861,000		25
Wood finishing	4,320,000	2,574,000		18
Support:				
Maintenance	-		25,200	9
Stores	-		15,120	3
Administration	-		10,080	12
Total	14,400,000	6,435,000	50,400	67

Overheads are allocated or apportioned on the most appropriate basis. The total overheads of the support cost centres are then reapportioned to the two production centres using the direct method.

- 70% of the Maintenance cost centre's time is spent maintaining production machinery in the Wood cutting production centre and the remainder in the Wood finishing production centre.

- The Stores cost centre makes 65% of its issues to the Wood cutting production centre, and 35% to the Wood finishing production centre.

- Administration supports the two production centres equally.

There is no reciprocal servicing between the three support cost centres.

Complete the overhead analysis table below:

	Basis of apportionment	Wood cutting £	Wood Finishing £	Maintenance £	Stores £	Admin £	Totals £
Depreciation of plant and equipment							
Power for production machinery							
Rent and rates							
Light and heat							
Indirect labour							
Totals							
Reapportion Maintenance							
Reapportion Stores							
Reapportion Admin.							
Total overheads to production centres							

34   AQUARIOUS

Aquarious Ltd's budgeted overheads for the next financial year are:

	£	£
Depreciation of plant and equipment		700,000
Power for production machinery		620,000
Rent and rates		100,000
Light and heat		20,000
Indirect labour costs:		
Maintenance	102,000	
Stores	40,000	
Administration	240,000	
Total indirect labour cost		382,000

The following information is also available:

Department	Net book value of plant and equipment.	Production machinery power usage (KwH)	Floor space (square metres)	Number of employees
Production:				
Assembly	4,440,000	2,210,000		10
Finishing	2,960,000	1,190,000		10
Support:				
Maintenance			12,000	6
Stores			8,000	4
Administration			5,000	8
Total	7,400,000	3,400,000	25,000	38

Overheads are allocated or apportioned on the most appropriate basis. The total overheads of the support cost centres are then reapportioned to the two production centres using the direct method.

- The overhead allocated and apportioned to Administration is re-apportioned to the other production and support cost centres based on the number of employees.

- The Stores cost centre makes 50% of its issues to the Assembly production centre, 30% to the Finishing production centre and 20% to Maintenance.

- 75% of the Maintenance cost centre's time is spent maintaining production machinery in the Assembly production centre and the remainder in the Finishing production centre.

Complete the overhead analysis table below:

	Basis of apportionment	Assembly £	Finishing £	Maintenance £	Stores £	Admin £	Totals £
Depreciation of plant and equipment							
Power for production machinery							
Rent and rates							
Light and heat							
Indirect labour							
Totals							
Reapportion Admin.							
Reapportion Stores							
Reapportion Maintenance							
Total overheads to production centres							

35 F4L has budgeted for the following overheads for its two profit and three cost centres for quarter 1 of the next financial year:

	£000	£000
Depreciation of aircraft		36,400
Aviation fuel and other variable costs		42,200
Pilots and aircrew salaries:		
Scheduled services	5,250	
Charter flights	4,709	
Total pilots and aircrew salaries		9,959
Rent and rates and other premises costs		12,600
Indirect labour costs:		
Aircraft maintenance and repairs	9,600	
Fuel and parts store	3,200	
General administration	7,800	
Total indirect labour cost		20,600

The following information is also available:

Profit/cost centre	Net book value of aircraft (£000)	Planned number of miles flown	Floor space (square metres)	Number of employees
Scheduled services	1,080,000	215,600		105
Charter flights	720,000	176,400		96
Aircraft maintenance and			190,000	260
Fuel and parts store			114,000	146
General administration			76,000	220
Total	1,800,000	392,000	380,000	827

Primary allocations or apportionments are made on the most appropriate basis. The support cost centres are then reapportioned to the two flight profit centres using the direct method.

- The Aircraft maintenance and repairs cost centre spends 60% of its time maintaining the aircraft in the scheduled services profit centre and the remainder in the charter flights profit centre.
- 55% of the issues from the Fuel and parts store cost centre is made to the scheduled services profit centre and the remainder to the charter flights profit centre.
- The scheduled services profit centre and the charter flights profit centre both incur general administration costs equally.
- The three support cost centres are not involved in reciprocal servicing.

Use the following table to allocate or apportion the overheads between the profit/cost centres, using the most appropriate basis.

	Basis of apportionment	Scheduled services £000	Charter flights £000	Aircraft maintenance and repairs £000	Fuel and parts store £000	General admin. £000	Totals £000
Depreciation of aircraft							
Aviation fuel and other variable costs							
Pilots and aircrew salaries							
Rent and rates and other premises costs							
Indirect labour							
Totals							
Reapportion Aircraft maintenance and repairs							
Reapportion Fuel and parts store							
Reapportion General admin.							
Total overheads to profit centres							

36   Premier Labels Ltd produces labelled plastic food containers. The budgeted overheads for the next quarter are shown below, together with their behaviour and how they are apportioned to departments.

Budgeted cost	Cost behaviour	£	Comments
Heat and lighting	Semi-variable	60,000	Apportion fixed element of £24,000 equally between all four departments. Apportion variable element according to floor area.
Power for machinery	Variable	28,000	Apportion 70% to Plastics Moulding, and 30% to Labelling.
Supervision	Fixed	120,000	Apportion to the two production departments pro rata to direct labour costs.
Stores wages	Fixed	72,000	
Equipment Maintenance salaries	Fixed	188,200	
Depreciation of non-current assets	Fixed	84,000	Apportion according to net book value of non-current assets.
Other overhead costs	Dependant on specific cost	128,000	Apportion 60% to Plastics Moulding, 20% to Labelling, and 10% each to Stores and Equipment Maintenance.

The following information is also available:

Department	Square metres occupied	Net book value of non-current assets (£)	Number of material requisitions	Direct labour costs (£)
Plastics Moulding	320,000	160,000	162,750	100,000
Labelling	180,000	80,000	56,000	140,000
Stores	80,000	30,000		
Equipment Maintenance	20,000	10,000		

Note:

The Equipment Maintenance department's total costs should be apportioned equally to the other three departments. Then the total of the Stores department's costs should be apportioned according to the number of material requisitions.

Complete the overhead analysis table below:

	Basis of apportionment	Plastics Moulding	Labelling	Stores	Equipment Maintenance	Totals
Heat and lighting fixed cost						
Heat and lighting variable cost						
Power for machinery						
Supervision						
Stores wages						
Equipment maintenance salaries						
Depreciation of non-current assets						
Other overhead costs						
Totals						
Reapportion Equipment maintenance						
Reapportion stores						
Total overheads to profit centres						

OVERHEAD ABSORPTION

37   **An overhead absorption rate is used to:**

   A   share out common costs over benefiting cost centres

   B   find the total overheads for a cost centre

   C   charge overheads to products

   D   control overheads

38   Cartcycle Ltd's budgeted overheads in the wood cutting department were £586,792. The overheads are absorbed based on machine hours. The budgeted machine hours were 9,464 and the actual machine hours were 9,745. The actual overhead cost was £568,631

   (a)   **What is the overhead absorption rate?**

      A   £62 per machine hour

      B   £60 per machine hour

      C   £58 per machine hour

      D   £55 per machine hour

   (b)   **How much overhead was absorbed?**

      A   £584,700

      B   £586,768

      C   £604,190

      D   £565,210

   (c)   **What is the under or over absorbed amount?**

      A   £35,559 over

      B   £35,599 under

      C   £21,582 over

      D   £21,582 under

39   Next quarter Aquarious Ltd's budgeted overheads and activity levels are:

	Assembly	Finishing
Budgeted overheads (£)	155,000	105,000
Budgeted direct labour hours	12,500	8,750
Budgeted machine hours	2,000	1,750

(a) **What would the budgeted overhead absorption rate be for each department, if this were set based on their both being heavily automated?**

    A   Assembly £77.50/hour, Finishing £12/hour

    B   Assembly £77.50/hour, Finishing £60/hour

    C   Assembly £12.40/hour, Finishing £60/hour

    D   Assembly £12.40/hour, Finishing £12/hour

(b) **What would the budgeted overhead absorption rate be for each department, if this were set based on their both being labour intensive?**

    A   Assembly £77.50/hour, Finishing £12/hour

    B   Assembly £77.50/hour, Finishing £60/hour

    C   Assembly £12.40/hour, Finishing £60/hour

    D   Assembly £12.40/hour, Finishing £12/hour

Additional data

At the end of the quarter actual overheads incurred were found to be:

	Assembly	Finishing
Actual overheads (£)	132,000	119,000

(c) **Assuming that exactly the same amount of overheads was absorbed as budgeted what were the budgeted under or over absorptions in the quarter?**

    A   Assembly over absorbed £23,000, Finishing over absorbed £14,000

    B   Assembly over absorbed £23,000, Finishing under absorbed £14,000

    C   Assembly under absorbed £23,000, Finishing under absorbed £14,000

    D   Assembly under absorbed £23,000, Finishing over absorbed £14,000

40 Next quarter Grape Limited's budgeted overheads and activity levels are:

	Moulding Dept	Painting Dept
Budgeted overheads (£)	36,000	39,000
Budgeted direct labour hours	9,000	13,000
Budgeted machine hours	18,000	1,200

(a) **What would the budgeted overhead absorption rate be for each department, if the most appropriate basis was chosen?**

    A   Moulding £2/hour, Painting £32.50/hour

    B   Moulding £32.50/hour, Painting £2/hour

    C   Moulding £3/hour, Painting £33/hour

    D   Moulding £2/hour, Painting £3/hour

Additional data

At the end of the quarter actual overheads incurred were found to be:

	Moulding Dept	Painting Dept
Actual overheads (£)	37,500	40,000
Actual direct labour hours	9,500	13,500
Actual machine hours	17,500	700

(b) **How much overhead has been absorbed by each department?**

    A   Moulding £35,000, Painting £40,500

    B   Moulding £37,500 Painting £40,000

    C   Moulding £19,000, Painting £2,100

    D   Moulding £36,000, Painting £39,000

(c) **Using your answer from b what are the under or over absorptions in the quarter?**

    A   Moulding over absorbed £2,500, Painting over absorbed £500

    B   Moulding under absorbed £2,500, Painting over absorbed £500

    C   Moulding over absorbed £2,500, Painting under absorbed £500

    D   Moulding under absorbed £2,500, Painting under absorbed £500

41   Next quarter Globe Limited's budgeted overheads and activity levels are:

	Mixing Dept	Bagging Dept
Budgeted overheads (£)	64,800	70,200
Budgeted direct labour hours	1,620	2,340
Actual direct labour hours	1,840	2,120
Budgeted machine hours	10,000	12,000
Actual machine hours	9,000	13,000

(a) **What would the budgeted overhead absorption rate for each department, if the mixing department was heavily automated and the bagging department was labour intensive?**

    A   Mixing £6.48/hour, Bagging £30.00/hour

    B   Mixing £7.20/hour, Bagging £33.11/hour

    C   Mixing £6.48/hour, Bagging £5.85/hour

    D   Mixing £5.00/hour, Bagging £5.00/hour

(b) **How much overhead has been absorbed by production in each department?**

    A   Mixing £13,248, Bagging £70,193

    B   Mixing £58,320, Bagging £76,050

    C   Mixing £58,320, Bagging £63,600

    D   Mixing £64,800, Bagging £70,200

Additional data

At the end of the quarter actual overheads incurred were found to be:

	Mixing Dept	Bagging Dept
Actual overheads (£)	67,500	75,600

(c)   **Using your answer from b what are the under or over absorptions in the quarter?**

A   Mixing under absorbed £9,180, Bagging over absorbed £12,000

B   Mixing under absorbed £9,180, Bagging under absorbed £12,000

C   Mixing over absorbed £9,180, Bagging over absorbed £12,000

D   Mixing over absorbed £9,180, Bagging under absorbed £12,000

42   **Over-absorbed overheads occur when:**

A   absorbed overheads exceed actual overheads

B   absorbed overheads exceed budgeted overheads

C   actual overheads exceed budgeted overheads

D   budgeted overheads exceed absorbed overheads

43   **The management accountant's report shows that fixed production overheads were over-absorbed in the last accounting period. The combination that is certain to lead to this situation is:**

A   production volume is lower than budget and actual expenditure is higher than budget

B   production volume is higher than budget and actual expenditure is higher than budget

C   production volume and actual cost are as budgeted

D   production volume is higher than budget and actual expenditure is lower than budget

44   **At the end of a period, in an integrated cost and financial accounting system, the accounting entries for £10,000 overheads over-absorbed would be:**

A	Dr	Work-in-progress control account	Cr	Overhead control account
B	Dr	Income statement	Cr	Work-in-progress control account
C	Dr	Income statement	Cr	Overhead control account
D	Dr	Overhead control account	Cr	Income statement

45   **During a period £50,000 was incurred for indirect labour. In a typical cost ledger, the double entry for this is:**

A	Dr	Wages control	Cr	Overhead control
B	Dr	WIP control	Cr	Wages control
C	Dr	Overhead control	Cr	Wages control
D	Dr	Wages control	Cr	WIP control

PROCESS COSTING

LOSSES

46   The Wood finishing department of Cartcyle Ltd uses process costing for some of its products.

The process account for July for one particular process has been partly completed but the following information is also relevant:

Two employees worked on this process during July. Each employee worked 40 hours per week for 4 weeks and was paid £18 per hour.

Overheads are absorbed on the basis of £28.80 per labour hour.

Cartcyle Ltd expects a normal loss of 5% during this process, which it then sells for scrap at £1.08 per kg.

Complete the process account below for July. Show total costs to the nearest £ and unit costs to 3 decimal places

Description	Kgs	Unit cost £	Total cost £		Description	Kgs	Unit cost £	Total cost £
Material TR	1,080	2.16			Normal loss		1.08	
Material DG	720	2.70			Output	2,300		
Material IG	720	1.10						
Labour								
Overheads								

47   **In process costing, if an abnormal loss arises the process account is generally:**

A   debited with the scrap value of the abnormal loss units

B   debited with the full production cost of the abnormal loss units

C   credited with the scrap value of the abnormal loss units

D   credited with the full production cost of the abnormal loss units

48 The metal finishing department of Aquarius Ltd uses process costing for some of its products.

The process account for December for one particular process has been partly completed but the following information is also relevant:

Two employees worked on this process during December. Each employee worked 40 hours per week for 4 weeks and was paid £8 per hour.

Overheads are absorbed on the basis of £12 per labour hour.

Aquarius Ltd expects a normal loss of 2% during this process, which it then sells for scrap at 50p per kg.

(a) **Complete the process account for December. Show total costs to the nearest £ and unit costs to 2 decimal places**

Description	Kgs	Unit cost £	Total cost £		Description	Kgs	Unit cost £	Total cost £
Material CBB	700	1.30			Normal loss		0.50	
Material BSS	500	1.12			Output	1,600		
Material SMA	500	0.72						
Labour								
Overheads								

(b) **Identify the correct entry for each of the following in a process account.**

	Debit	Credit
Abnormal loss		
Abnormal gain		

49 The Glazing department of Grape Ltd uses process costing for glazing finished statues.

The process account for January for one particular process has been partly completed but the following information is also relevant:

Four employees worked on this process during January. Each employee worked 30 hours per week for 4 weeks and was paid £12 per hour.

Overheads are absorbed on the basis of £8 per labour hour.

Grape Ltd expects a normal loss of 10% during this process, which it then sells for scrap at £5 per kg.

Complete the process account below for January. Show total costs to the nearest £ and unit costs to 2 decimal places

Description	Units	Unit cost £	Total cost £		Description	Units	Unit cost £	Total cost £
Input – Statues	300	11.25	3,375		Normal loss		5.00	
Materials – Glaze			500		Output	290		
Labour								
Overheads								

50   Last month one of CPL's products had the following process inputs:

- Direct materials   500 kgs at £17.20 per kg
- Direct labour   280 labour hours at £10.50 per hour
- Overheads absorbed   86 machine hours at £32 per machine hour

The following information is also available:

- The company expects a normal loss of 5% of input.
- All waste is sold for £1.68 per kg.
- Actual output for the month was 515 kgs.
- There were no opening or closing stocks and all output was fully completed.

(a)   **Calculate the product's cost per kg of normal production.**

> £   per kg

(b)   **Prepare the process account below for the product for last month:**

Description	Kgs	Unit cost £	Total cost £		Description	Kgs	Unit cost £	Total cost £
Materials					Output			
Labour					Normal loss			
Overheads								

EQUIVALENT UNITS

51 Bahadra makes biscuits. Production requires several successive processes and the production details of the first process are as follows.

Volume completed in period	5,000 kg
Closing work in process	600 kg

Degree of completion of closing WIP:

Materials	100%
Labour	50%
Overheads	50%

Costs incurred in April:

Materials	£56,000
Labour	£26,500
Overheads	£10,600

Complete the table below and value the completed output and CWIP

Statement of EU

	Materials	*Conversion*
Completed		
CWIP		
TOTAL EU		
Costs		
Period Costs		
TOTAL COSTS		
Cost per EU		

Valuation of Completed Output	£
Valuation of CWIP	£

52 Parry makes bungee cords. Production requires several successive processes and the production details of the first process are as follows.

Volume completed in period	9,000 units
Closing work in process	3,500 units

Degree of completion of closing WIP:

Materials	100%
Labour	75%
Overheads	75%

Costs incurred in April:

Materials	£18,750
Labour	£12,415
Overheads	£16,415

The valuation of the completed output is:

A £11,760

B £34,258

C £35,820

D £47,580

53 The following data relates to work in progress stocks of solvent S789 during November:

Opening work in progress	Nil
Finished output to next process	7,000 litres
Closing work in progress	1,200 litres
Degree of completion – direct materials	100%
Degree of completion – direct labour	50%

The total labour cost is £3,800.

The direct labour cost per litre of solvent S789 of the equivalent finished production is:

A £0.46

B £0.50

C £0.60

D £0.63

54 Diamond makes graphite pencils on a production line. The details of the process in Period 2 are as follows:

Opening WIP = 250 units

Costs incurred so far (i.e. value of opening WIP)

Materials	£54,000	
Conversion	£42,000	

Degrees of completion

Materials	100%	
Conversion	60%	

Completed output = 3,200 units

Costs incurred in Period 2:

Materials	£123,900	
Conversion	£91,500	

Calculate the cost per equivalent unit using the FIFO method of valuing WIP

Equivalent units		Material	Conversion
	OWIP to complete		
	Completed Output		
	Total EU		
Costs			
	Period		
	Total cost		
Cost per EU			

55 Squid makes fountain pens on a production line. The details of the process in Period 2 are as follows:

Opening WIP = 400 units

Costs incurred so far

Materials	£115	
Conversion	£270	

Degrees of completion

Materials	100%	
Conversion	60%	

Completed output = 800 units

Costs incurred in Period 2:

Materials	£212	
Conversion	£448	

The cost per equivalent unit for materials and conversion using the FIFO method of valuing WIP:

	Materials	Conversion
A	£0.27	£0.47
B	£0.53	£0.70
C	£0.53	£0.80
D	£0.82	£1.28

56 Silver makes key rings on a production line. The details of the process in period 2 are as follows:

OWIP =   250 units

Costs incurred so far

	Materials	£53,800
	Conversion	£42,000

Degrees of completion

	Materials	100%
	Conversion	60%

Completed output =   3,200 units

Costs incurred in Period 2:

	Materials	£135,000
	Conversion	£98,800

Calculate the cost per equivalent unit using the AVCO method of valuing WIP

Equivalent units		Material	Conversion
	Completed Output		
	Total EU		
Costs			
	OWIP		
	Period		
	Total cost		
Cost per EU			

57 A factory manufactures fizzy drinks. During October work commenced on 11,000 litres.

OWIP = 2,000 litres

Costs incurred so far

Materials	£400
Conversion	£150

Degrees of completion

Materials	100%
Conversion	50%

Completed output = 9,000 litres

Costs incurred in Period:

Materials	£950
Conversion	£750

The cost per equivalent unit for materials and conversion using AVCO to value OWIP are:

	Material	Conversion
A	£6.67	£10
B	£6.67	£11
C	£0.15	£0.09
D	£0.15	£0.10

BASIC VARIANCE ANALYSIS

58 **Which of the following statements are correct?**

(i) An adverse variance increases profit

(ii) A favourable variance increases profit

(iii) A favourable variance will arise when actual revenue is greater than budgeted revenue

(iv) An adverse variance will arise when actual costs are greater than budgeted costs

Options:

A (i) only

B (ii) only

C (i), (iii) and (iv)

D (ii), (iii) and (iv)

59 Aquarius Ltd. has the following original budget and actual performance for product Britz for the year ending 31 December.

	Budget	Actual
Volume sold	200,000	267,000
	£000	£000
Sales revenue	1,600	2,409
Less costs:		
Direct materials	400	801
Direct labour	200	267
Overheads	600	750
Operating profit	400	591

Both direct materials and direct labour are variable costs, but the overheads are fixed

Complete the table below to show a flexed budget and the resulting variances against this budget for the year. Show the actual variance amount, for sales and each cost, in the column headed 'Variance' and indicate whether this is Favourable or Adverse by entering F or A in the final column. If neither F nor A enter 0.

	Flexed Budget	Actual	Variance	Favourable F or Adverse A
Volume sold		267,000		
	£000	£000	£000	
Sales revenue		2,409		
Less costs:				
Direct materials		801		
Direct labour		267		
Overheads		750		
Operating profit		591		

60 Grape Ltd. has the following original budget and actual performance for product Bird Box Sets for the year ending 31 December.

	Budget	Actual
Volume sold	20,000	28,800
	£000	£000
Sales revenue	3,000	3,877
Less costs:		
Direct materials	175	212
Direct labour	875	912
Overheads	445	448
Operating profit	1,505	2,305

Both direct materials and direct labour are variable costs, but the overheads are fixed

Complete the table below to show a flexed budget and the resulting variances against this budget for the year. Show the actual variance amount, for sales and each cost, in the column headed 'Variance' and indicate whether this is Favourable or Adverse by entering F or A in the final column. If neither F nor A enter 0.

	Flexed Budget	Actual	Variance	Favourable F or Adverse A
Volume sold		28,800		
	£000	£000	£000	
Sales revenue		3,877		
Less costs:				
Direct materials		212		
Direct labour		912		
Overheads		448		
Operating profit		2,305		

61 Globe Ltd. has the following original budget and actual performance for product Bean for the year ending 31 December.

	Budget	Actual
Volume sold (litres)	4,000	5,000
	£000	£000
Sales revenue	1,500	1,950
Less costs:		
Direct materials	36	45
Direct labour	176	182
Overheads	89	90
Operating profit	1,199	1,633

Both direct materials and direct labour are variable costs, but the overheads are fixed

Complete the table below to show a flexed budget and the resulting variances against this budget for the year. Show your answer to the nearest £1000. Show the actual variance amount, for sales and each cost, in the column headed 'Variance' and indicate whether this is Favourable or Adverse by entering F or A in the final column. If neither F nor A enter 0.

	Flexed Budget	Actual	Variance	Favourable F or Adverse A
Volume sold		5,000		
	£000	£000	£000	
Sales revenue		1,950		
Less costs:				
Direct materials		45		
Direct labour		182		
Overheads		90		
Operating profit		1,633		

SHORT TERM DECISION MAKING

COST VOLUME PROFIT ANALYSIS

62 Product MR13 has a selling price of £41.40 per unit with a total variable cost of £27 per unit. Cartcyle Ltd estimates that the fixed costs per quarter associated with this product are £64,800.

(a) **Calculate the budgeted breakeven point, in units, for product MR13.**

units

(b) **Calculate the budgeted breakeven revenue, in £s, for product MR13.**

£

(c) **Complete the table below to show the budgeted margin of safety in units and the margin of safety percentage if Cartcyle Ltd sells 9,000 units or 10,800 units of product MR13.**

Units of MR13 sold	9,000	10,800
Margin of safety (units)		
Margin of safety percentage (2dp)		

(d) **If Cartcyle Ltd wishes to make a profit of £36,000, how many units of MR13 must it sell?**

units

(e) **If Cartcyle Ltd increases the selling price of MR13 by £1.80 what will be the impact on the breakeven point and the margin of safety assuming no change in the number of units sold?**

A   The breakeven point will decrease and the margin of safety will increase

B   The breakeven point will stay the same but the margin of safety will decrease

C   The breakeven point will decrease and the margin of safety will stay the same

D   The breakeven point will increase and the margin of safety will decrease

63 Seafood soup sells for 80p per can. It has a marginal cost of production of 30p per can. Fixed costs attributable to this range of soups total £312,500.

(a) **Calculate the sales revenue of seafood soup CCS has to achieve to break even.**

£ _____

(b) **Calculate the sales revenue of seafood soup CCS needs to achieve to make a profit of £200,000.**

£ _____

(c) **If CCS were to sell £875,000 worth of seafood soup, what would be:**

(i) **the margin of safety**

£ _____

(ii) **the margin of safety percentage over the break-even sales?**

_____ %

64 The following budgeted annual sales and cost information relates to labelled food containers types A and B:

Product	A	B
Units made and sold	300,000	500,000
Machine hours required	60,000	40,000
Sales revenue (£)	450,000	600,000
Direct materials (£)	60,000	125,000
Direct labour (£)	36,000	70,000
Variable overheads (£)	45,000	95,000

Total fixed costs attributable to A and B are budgeted to be £264,020.

(a) **Complete the table below (to 2 decimal places) to show the budgeted contribution per unit of A and B sold, and the company's budgeted profit or loss for the year from these two products.**

	A (£)	B (£)	Total (£)
Selling price per unit			
Less: variable costs per unit			
Direct materials			
Direct labour			
Variable overheads			
Contribution per unit			
Sales volume (units)			
Total contribution			
Less: fixed costs			
Budgeted profit or loss			

The £264,020 of fixed costs attributed to products A and B can be split between the two products: £158,620 to A and £105,400 to B.

The latest sales forecast is that 250,000 units of product A and 400,000 units of product B will be sold during the year.

(b) **Using your calculations and the additional data above, complete the table below to calculate:**

Product	A	B
Fixed costs (£)		
Unit contribution (£)		
Break-even sales (units)		
Forecast sales (units)		
Margin of safety (units)		
Margin of safety (%)		

(c) **Which of the 2 products has the safer margin of safety?**

Product A		Product B	

65 Eastern Bus Company (ECB) has produced three forecasts of miles to be driven during the next three months for a particular contract. The original contract is for journeys totalling 10,000 miles. It now seems likely, however, that the total journeys involved will increase to either 12,000 or 14,000 miles.

(a) **Complete the table below in order to estimate the profit per mile (in pounds, to 3 decimal places) of this contract for the three likely mileages.**

Likely miles	10,000	12,000	14,000
	£	£	£
Sales revenue	100,000		
Variable costs:			
• Fuel	8,000		
• Drivers' wages and associated costs	5,000		
• Overheads	6,000		
Fixed costs:			
• Indirect labour	10,600		
• Overheads	25,850		
Total cost	55,450		
Total profit	44,550		
Profit per mile	4.455		

(b) **Using the information provided above and your own calculations for that task, calculate:**

Forecast number of miles		12,000	14,000
Sales revenue	£		
Fixed costs	£		
Contribution	£		
Contribution per mile	£		
Break-even number of miles	Miles		
Break-even sales revenue	£		
Margin of safety in number of miles	Miles		
Margin of safety in sales revenue	£		
Margin of safety	%		

66   Four lines representing expected costs and revenues have been drawn on a breakeven chart:

Match the line letter with the correct description?

A
B
C
D

Fixed costs
Total revenue
Total costs
Total variable costs

LIMITING FACTOR ANALYSIS

67   A company manufactures two products (L and M) using the same material and labour. It holds no inventory. Information about the variable costs and maximum demands are as follows:

	Product L	Product M
Material (litre)	3.25	4.75
Labour (hour)	5	4
Maximum monthly demand (units)	6,000	8,000

Each month 50,000 litres of material and 60,000 labour hours are available.

Which one of the following statements is correct?

A   Material is a limiting factor but labour is not a limiting factor

B   Material is not a limiting factor but labour is a limiting factor

C   Neither material nor labour is a limiting factor

D   Both material and labour are limiting factors

68   Yeknom makes two products, the apple breakfast bar and the banana breakfast bar. The
following budgeted annual sales and cost information relates to a and b:

Product	Apple bars	Banana bars
Bars made and sold	75,000	125,000
Machine hours required	30,000	20,000
Sales revenue(£)	225,000	300,000
Direct materials (£)	30,000	62,500
Direct labour (£)	18,000	35,000
Variable overheads (£)	22,500	47,500
Fixed overheads (£)	150,000	

(a)   **Complete the table below (to 2 decimal places) to show the budgeted contribution
per bar of Apple and bar of Banana sold, and the company's budgeted profit or loss
for the year from these two products.**

	Apple (£)	Banana (£)	Total (£)
Selling price per bar			
Less: variable costs per unit			
Direct materials			
Direct labour			
Variable overheads			
Contribution per unit			
Sales volume (bars)			
Total contribution			
Less: fixed costs			
Budgeted profit or loss			

Due to a machine breakdown the number of machine hours available for products Apple
bars and Banana bars has now been reduced to only 35,000 during the year.

(b)   **Given this limitation and your calculations, complete the table below to recommend how many bars of products Apple and Banana Yeknom should now make in order to maximise the profit from these two products for the year.**

Product	Apple bars	Banana bars	Total
Contribution/unit (£)			
Machine hours/unit			
Contribution/machine hour (£)			
Product ranking			
Machine hours available			
Machine hours allocated to: Product .... Product			
Units made			
Total contribution			
Less: fixed costs (£)			
Profit/loss made (£)			

69   Monty makes two products, the Squeaker and the Hooter. The following budgeted annual sales and cost information relates to the Squeaker and the Hooter:

Product	Squeaker	Hooter
Units made and sold	80,000	70,000
Machine hours required	40,000	17,500
Sales revenue(£)	100,000	122,500
Direct materials (£)	40,000	17,500
Direct labour (£)	20,000	35,000
Variable overheads (£)	20,000	45,500
Fixed overheads (£)	15,000	

(a)   **Complete the table below (to 2 decimal places) to show the budgeted contribution per bar of Squeakers and Hooters sold, and the company's budgeted profit or loss for the year from these two products.**

	Squeaker (£)	Hooter (£)	Total (£)
Selling price per bar			
Less: variable costs per unit			
Direct materials			
Direct labour			
Variable overheads			
Contribution per unit			
Sales volume (bars)			
Total contribution			
Less: fixed costs			
Budgeted profit or loss			

Due to a machine breakdown the number of machine hours available for production has now been reduced to only 50,000 during the year.

(b)   **Given this limitation and your calculations, complete the table below to recommend how many units of Squeakers and Hooters Monty should now make in order to maximise the profit from these two products for the year.**

Product	Squeakers	Hooters	Total
Contribution/unit (£)			
Machine hours/unit			
Contribution/machine hour (£)			
Product ranking			
Machine hours available			
Machine hours allocated to: Product .... Product			
Units made			
Total contribution			
Less: fixed costs (£)			
Profit/loss made (£)			

70 Three of CPL's products use the same rare plant extract as part of their manufacture. The sole supplier has informed CPL that, due to flooding at its South American facility, they can only supply 6,000 kgs of the plant extract next month.

The following is the budget information about the three affected products for next month:

Product	AB1	CD2	EF3	Total
	£	£	£	£
Contribution	26,400	34,600	48,204	109,204
Fixed costs allocated or apportioned	7,430	9,750	13,600	30,780
Profit	18,970	24,850	34,604	78,424
Number of packs to be sold	6,600	6,920	16,068	
Kgs of plant extract required	2,640	1,730	8,034	

Complete the table below to advise how many packs of each product should actually be produced next month to maximise profits during this period.

Product	AB1	CD2	EF3	Total
Contribution/pack (£)				
Kgs of plant extract/pack				
Contribution/kg (£)				
Product ranking				
Kgs of plant extract available				
Kgs allocated to each product				
Number of packs to produce				
Total contribution earned (£)				
Less: Fixed costs (£)				
Profit/loss made (£)				

71   Asparagus soup and broccoli soup have the following budgeted annual sales and cost information:

Product	Asparagus soup	Broccoli soup
Cans made and sold	1,200,000	1,800,000
Machine hours required	6,000	9,000
Sales revenue (£)	720,000	900,000
Direct materials (£)	84,000	108,000
Direct labour (£)	72,000	126,000
Variable overheads (£)	24,000	54,000
Fixed overheads attributable to both types	652,000	

(a)   **Complete the table below (in pence) to show the budgeted contribution per can for both types of soup, and the company's budgeted profit or loss for the year from these two products (in £).**

	Asparagus soup	Broccoli soup	
	p	p	
Selling price per can			
Less: variable costs per can			
Direct materials			
Direct labour			
Variable overheads			
Contribution per can			
	No of cans	No of cans	
Sales volume (cans)			
	£	£	Total (£)
Total contribution			
Less: fixed costs			
Budgeted profit or loss			

Due to a machine breakdown the number of machine hours available for production has now been reduced to only 12,000 during the year.

(b) **Given this limitation and your calculations, complete the table below to recommend how many cans of Asparagus soup and Broccoli soup CPL should now make in order to maximise the profit from these two products for the year.**

Product	Asparagus soup	Broccoli soup	Total
Contribution/can (£)			
Machine hours/can			
Contribution/machine hour (£)			
Product ranking			
Machine hours available			
Machine hours allocated to: Product .... Product			
Units made			
Total contribution			
Less: fixed costs (£)			
Profit/loss made (£)			

LONG TERM DECISION MAKING

NPV AND PAYBACK

72 One of the finishing machines in Cartcycle Ltd's Wood finishing department is nearing the end of its useful life and the company is considering purchasing a replacement machine.

Estimates have been made for the initial capital cost, sales income and operating costs of the replacement machine, which is expected to have a useful life of three years:

	Year 0 £000	Year 1 £000	Year 2 £000	Year 3 £000
Capital expenditure	1,620			
Other cash flows:				
Sales income		756	1,008	1,440
Operating costs		216	270	342

The company appraises capital investment projects using a 15% cost of capital.

(a) **Complete the table below and calculate the net present value of the proposed replacement machine (to the nearest £000).**

	Year 0 £000	Year 1 £000	Year 2 £000	Year 3 £000
Capital expenditure				
Sales income				
Operating costs				
Net cash flows				
PV factors	1.0000	0.8696	0.7561	0.6575
Discounted cash flows				
Net present value				

The net present value is *of positive/negative**

*delete as appropriate

(b) **Calculate the payback of the proposed replacement machine to the nearest whole month.**

The payback period is   ---------- Year(s) and   ------------ Months

73 One of the finishing machines in Aquarius Ltd's metal finishing department is nearing the end of its useful life and the company is considering purchasing a replacement machine.

Estimates have been made for the initial capital cost, sales income and operating costs of the replacement machine, which is expected to have a useful life of three years:

	Year 0 £000	Year 1 £000	Year 2 £000	Year 3 £000
Capital expenditure	1,200			
Other cash flows:				
Sales income		530	570	710
Operating costs		140	160	170

The company appraises capital investment projects using a 15% cost of capital.

(a) **Complete the table below and calculate the net present value of the proposed replacement machine (to the nearest £000).**

	Year 0 £000	Year 1 £000	Year 2 £000	Year 3 £000
Capital expenditure				
Sales income				
Operating costs				
Net cash flows				
PV factors	1.0000	0.8696	0.7561	0.6575
Discounted cash flows				
Net present value				

The net present value is *positive/negative**

delete as appropriate

(b) **If the net cash inflow in year 4 was £530,000, calculate the payback of the proposed replacement machine to the nearest whole month.**

The payback period is ---------- Year(s) and ------------ Months

74 One of the moulding machines in Grape Ltd's Moulding department is nearing the end of its useful life and the company is considering purchasing a replacement machine.

Estimates have been made for the initial capital cost, sales income and operating costs of the replacement machine, which is expected to have a useful life of three years:

	Year 0 £000	Year 1 £000	Year 2 £000	Year 3 £000
Capital expenditure	500			
Other cash flows:				
Sales income		280	330	370
Operating costs		100	120	140

The company appraises capital investment projects using a 10% cost of capital.

(a) **Complete the table below and calculate the net present value of the proposed replacement machine (to the nearest £000).**

	Year 0 £000	Year 1 £000	Year 2 £000	Year 3 £000
Capital expenditure				
Sales income				
Operating costs				
Net cash flows				
PV factors	1.0000	0.909	0.826	0.751
Discounted cash flows				
Net present value				

The net present value is *positive/negative**

*delete as appropriate

(b) **Calculate the payback of the proposed replacement machine to the nearest whole month.**

The payback period is ---------- Year(s) and ------------ Months

75 Bartrum Ltd is needs to purchase a new mashing machine. There are 2 machines available for purchase. Calculate the net present cost of each machine and recommend which machine should be purchased.

Machine A

	Year 0 £000	Year 1 £000	Year 2 £000	Year 3 £000
Capital expenditure	1,085			
Operating costs		200	200	200

Machine B

	Year 0 £000	Year 1 £000	Year 2 £000	Year 3 £000
Capital expenditure	1,200			
Operating costs		150	160	170

The company appraises capital investment projects using a 15% cost of capital.

Complete the tables below and calculate the net present cost of each of the proposed replacement machines (to the nearest £000).

Machine A

	Year 0 £000	Year 1 £000	Year 2 £000	Year 3 £000
Capital expenditure				
Operating costs				
Net cash flows				
PV factors	1.0000	0.8696	0.7561	0.6575
Discounted cash flows				
Net present cost				

Machine B

	Year 0 £000	Year 1 £000	Year 2 £000	Year 3 £000
Capital expenditure				
Operating costs				
Net cash flows				
PV factors	1.0000	0.8696	0.7561	0.6575
Discounted cash flows				
Net present cost				

Bartrum should invest in *Machine A/Machine B**

*delete as appropriate

76   CPL is considering replacing its fleet of delivery vehicles, and has produced the following estimates of capital expenditure and operating costs for two types of van. Both types of van are expected to have a three-year economic life.

Van type P	Year 0 £000	Year 1 £000	Year 2 £000	Year 3 £000
Capital expenditure	600			
Disposal proceeds				150
Operating costs		275	290	315

Van type R	Year 0 £000	Year 1 £000	Year 2 £000	Year 3 £000
Capital expenditure	750			
Disposal proceeds				170
Operating costs		345	365	390

The company's cost of capital is 16%.

Calculate the net present cost for both types of van. (Round the discounted cash flows to the nearest £000).

The net present cost of van type P

	Year 0 £000	Year 1 £000	Year 2 £000	Year 3 £000
Capital expenditure				
Disposal				
Operating costs				
Net cash flows				
PV factors	1.0000	0.8621	0.7432	0.6407
Discounted cash flows				
Net present cost				

The net present cost of van type R

	Year 0 £000	Year 1 £000	Year 2 £000	Year 3 £000
Capital expenditure/disposal				
Operating costs				
Net cash flows				
PV factors	1.0000	0.8621	0.7432	0.6407
Discounted cash flows				
Net present cost				

CPL should invest in *Van type P/Van type R**

*delete as appropriate

77 (a) **Globe Ltd's Finance Director has calculated an IRR of 12% for an investment opportunity. The company's required cost of capital is 15%. Should Globe Ltd take this investment opportunity?**

Yes/No

(b) **Globe Ltd's Finance Director has calculated an IRR of 17% for another investment opportunity. The companies required cost of capital is 15%. Should Globe Ltd take this investment opportunity?**

Yes/No

(c) **Globe Ltd's Finance Director has calculated an IRR of 15% for an investment opportunity. The companies required cost of capital is 15%. What is the value of the NPV?**

£

78 A company is considering investing in a new mixing machine that will cost £3,000,000 to purchase but will reduce operating costs of the company. The following information is relevant to this decision:

- The payback period would be 2.4 years. The company's policy is for projects to pay back within 3 years.
- The net present value is £400,000 negative.
- The internal rate of return is 14%. The company's cost of capital is 16%.

Complete the report below, deleting words/phases where appropriate (marked with *)

REPORT

To: The Chief Accountant

From: AAT student

Subject: Investment appraisal

Date: 3 December 20X2

The payback period of 2.4 years is *within/outside** the company's policy of 3 years, and on this criterion the investment *should go/should not go** ahead.

The NPV is *positive/negative** and on this criterion the investment *should go /should not go** ahead.

The IRR, at 14%, is *above/below** the company's 16% cost of capital and on this criterion the investment *should go/should not go** ahead.

Overall the investment *should/should not** proceed because the *Payback/NPV/IRR** is the dominant criterion.

Section 2

ANSWERS TO PRACTICE QUESTIONS

PRINCIPLES OF COST ACCOUNTING

COST BEHAVIOURS

1   C

	£
Total cost of 18,500 hours	251,750
Total cost of 17,000 hours	246,500
Variable cost of 1,500 hours	5,250

Variable cost per machine hour = £5,250/1,500 machine hours = £3.50.

	£
Total cost of 17,000 hours	246,500
Less variable cost of 17,000 hours (× £3.50)	59,500
Balance = fixed costs	187,000

2   A

	Cost per unit (£) (125 units)	Cost per unit (£) (180 units)
T1	8.00	7.00
T2	14.00	14.00
T3	19.80	15.70
T4	25.80	25.80

Cost types T2 and T4 are variable and T1 and T3 are semi-variable.

3   GRAPH 1 C; GRAPH 2 D

4   *Direct* costs are ones that can be economically and exclusively identified with a cost unit. Examples include *Fabric* used in production of clothing and *Electrical components* used in the manufacture of computers.

Indirect costs, or *Overheads*, are costs that cannot be economically and exclusively identified with a cost unit. Examples include *Light, heat and power costs*.

5

Batches produced and sold	2,160	2,700	3,600
	£	£	£
Sales revenue	64,800	81,000	108,000
Variable costs:			
• Direct materials	9,720	12,150	16,200
• Direct labour	22,680	28,350	37,800
• Overheads	12,960	16,200	21,600
Semi-variable costs:	6,804		
• Variable element		5,400	7,200
• Fixed element		2,484	2,484
Total cost	52,164	64,584	85,284
Total profit	12,636	16,416	22,716
Profit per batch (to 2 decimal places)	5.85	6.08	6.31

6

Likely miles	5,000	6,000	7,000
	£000	£000	£000
Sale revenue	2,500	2,950	3,400
Variable/semi-variable costs:			
• Aviation fuel	400	480	560
• Landing and servicing fees	850	900	950
• Other variable overheads	135	162	189
Fixed costs:			
• Wages and salaries	420	420	420
• Other fixed overheads	625	625	625
Total cost	2430	2,587	2,744
Total profit	70	363	656
Profit per mile flown (2 d.p.) £	14.00	60.50	93.71

7

Batches produced and sold	800	1,200	1,500
	£	£	£
Sales revenue	24,000	36,000	45,000
Variable costs:			
• Direct materials	3,600	5,400	6,750
• Direct labour	8,400	12,600	15,750
• Overheads	1,800	2,700	3,375
Semi-variable costs:	2,520		
• Variable element		3,600	4,500
• Fixed element		120	120
Total cost	16,320	24,420	30,495
Total profit	7,680	11,580	14,505
Profit per batch (to 2 decimal places)	9.60	9.65	9.67

MATERIAL COSTS

INVENTORY RECORDS

8   (a)   The EOQ = $\sqrt{\left(\frac{2 \times 3.60 \times 112,500}{1.80}\right)} = 671$

(b)   Inventory record card

	Receipts			Issues			Balance	
Date	Quantity kgs	Cost per kg (£)	Total cost (£)	Quantity kgs	Cost per kg (p)	Total cost (£)	Quantity kgs	Total cost (£)
Balance as at 22 July							198	238
24 July	671	2.336	1,567				869	1,805
26 July				540	1.920	1,037	329	768
28 July	671	2.344	1,573				1,000	2,341
30 July				710	2.341	1,662	290	679

Workings

Issue on 26th July is made up of 198 @ 1.202 and 342 @ 2.336

Issue on 30th July is made up of 329 @ 2.336 and 391 @ 2.344

9 (a) The EOQ = $\sqrt{\left(\frac{2 \times 2.50 \times 2,500 \times 12}{1.00}\right)} = 388$

(b) Inventory record card

Date	Receipts			Issues			Balance	
	Quantity litres	Cost per litre	Total cost (£)	Quantity litres	Cost per litre	Total cost (£)	Quantity Litres	Total cost (£)
Balance as at 23 June							65	130
24 June	388	2.234	867				453	997
26 June				180	2.201	397	273	600
27 June	388	2.341	909				661	1,509
30 June				250	2.283	571	411	938

10 (a) C – AVCO

(b) Inventory record card

Date	Receipts			Issues			Balance	
	Drums	Cost per Drum (£)	Total cost (£)	Drums	Cost per drum (p)	Total cost (£)	Drums	Total cost (£)
Balance as at 22 January							1,650	1,980
25 January	1,200	1.250	1,500				2,850	3,480
26 January				1,300	1.221	1,587	1,550	1,893
28 January	1,200	1.302	1,562				2,750	3,455
31 January				1,500	1.256	1,884	1,250	1,571

11 (a) A – FIFO

(b) Inventory record card

Date	Receipts			Issues			Balance	
	Tonnes	Cost per tonne (£)	Total cost (£)	Tonnes	Cost per tonne (£)	Total cost (£)	Tonnes	Total cost (£)
Balance as at 27 March							1,200	14,400
28 March	800	12.50	10,000				2,000	24,400
29 March				820	12.00	9,840	1,180	14,560
30 March	800	12.25	9,800				1,980	24,360
31 March				900	12.29	11,060	1,080	13,300

Working

Issue on 31st March is made up of 380 @ 12 and 520 @12.50

12 **A** – FIFO

13 **A**

When prices are rising, FIFO will give a higher valuation for closing inventory, because the closing inventory will consist of the most recently-purchased items. Higher closing inventory means lower cost of sales and higher profit.

MATERIAL BOOKKEEPING

14 **C**

Materials inventory account

	£000s		£000s
Opening inventory	15	Issued to production	165
Payables for purchases	176	Returned to suppliers	8
Returned to stores	9	Written off	4
		Closing balance (balancing item)	23
	200		200

15

	Choice
Transaction 1	(C) Dr. Inventory, Cr. Bank
Transaction 2	(F) Dr. Production, Cr. Inventory
Transaction 3	(D) Dr. Inventory, Cr. Trade payables' Control
Transaction 4	(E) Dr. Inventory, Cr. Production

16

	Choice
Transaction 1	(D) Dr. Inventory, Cr. Trade payables' Control
Transaction 2	(F) Dr. Income statement, Cr. Inventory
Transaction 3	(C) Dr. Inventory, Cr. Bank
Transaction 4	(B) Dr. Trade payables' Control, Cr. Inventory

17   B

Indirect materials are overhead costs so debit production overhead. An issue of materials is a credit from the material control account

LABOUR COSTS

TIME SHEETS

18   **Employee's weekly timesheet for week ending 7 December**

Employee: A. Man				**Profit Centre:** Wood finishing		
Employee number: C812				**Basic pay per hour:** £8.00		
	Hours spent on production	Hours worked on indirect work	Notes	Basic pay £	Overtime premium £	Total pay £
Monday	6	2	10am–12am cleaning of machinery	64	8	72
Tuesday	2	4	9am–1pm customer care course	48	0	48
Wednesday	8			64	8	72
Thursday	6			48	0	48
Friday	6	1	3–4pm health and safety training	56	4	60
Saturday	6			48	24	72
Sunday	3			24	24	48
Total	**37**	**7**		352	68	420

Alternative

Sunday	3			0	48	48
Total	**37**	**7**		328	92	420

19 (a)

	Units
Actual production	5,400,000
Standard production (5,000 hours at 800 units)	(4,000,000)
Excess production	1,400,000
Bonus %	25% × $\dfrac{1,400,000}{4,000,000}$ = 8.75%
Group bonus rate per hour	0.0875 × £10 = £0.875
Total group bonus	5,000 hours at £0.875 = £4,375

(b)   Basic pay 44 hours at £9.60 =   £422.40

Bonus pay 44 hours at £0.875 =   £38.50

Total pay   £460.90

20   **Employee's weekly timesheet for week ending 31 January**

Employee: Olivia Michael			Profit Centre: Moulding Department			
Employee number: P450			Basic pay per hour: £10.00			
	Hours spent in work	Hours worked on indirect work	Notes	Basic pay £	Overtime premium £	Total pay £
Monday	8	3	10am–1pm cleaning moulds	80	5	85.00
Tuesday	7	4	9am–1pm fire training	70	0	70.00
Wednesday	8			80	5	85.00
Thursday	7	1		70	0	70.00
Friday	7	1	3–4pm annual appraisal	70	0	70.00
Saturday	3			30	7.50	37.50
Total	**40**	**9**		400	17.50	417.50

Labour cost account

	£		£
Bank	417.50	Production	310
		Production Overheads	107.50

Production is direct labour only therefore basic hours less time spent on non-production activities:

$(40 − 9) × £10 = £310$

Production overheads are the indirect costs therefore the cost is:

$£17.50 + (9 × £10) = £107.50$

21 (a) The wages control account entries

Wages control account

	£		£
Bank (net wages/salaries)	10,000	Maintenance (direct labour)	7,000
HMRC (income tax and NIC)	2,000	Maintenance overheads	4,000
Pension contribution	1,000	Maintenance administration	2,000
	13,000		**13,000**

(b) The total payroll cost charged to the various cost accounts of the business

Date	Code	Debit	Credit
30 November	8200		7,000
30 November	6200	7,000	
30 November	8200		4,000
30 November	6400	4,000	
30 November	8200		2,000
30 November	6600	2,000	

22

	Choice
Transaction 1	(A) Dr. Wages control, Cr. Bank
Transaction 2	(B) Dr. Work-in-progress, Cr. Wages control
Transaction 3	(C) Dr. Production overhead account, Cr. Wages Control
Transaction 4	(D) Dr. Production overhead control, Cr. Bank

23 (a)   The correct total cost of direct labour for the bottles is:

Cost at normal rate:	1,215 hours at £8 =	£9,720
Cost at time and a half:	180 hours at £4 =	£720
Cost at double time:	135 hours at £8 =	£1,080
Total direct labour cost		£11,520

Alternative calculation:

Cost at normal rate:	900 hours at £8 =	£7,200
Cost at time and a half:	180 hours at £12 =	£2,160
Cost at double time:	135 hours at £16 =	£2,160
Total direct labour cost		£11,520

(b)   The cost of direct labour per bottle is:

Total direct labour cost:	£11,520
Divided by number of bottles	57,600
Cost of direct labour per bottle	£0.20

24   **C**

Product	Quantity	Standard time per item (hours)	Total Standard time (hours)
Buckles	50	0.2	10
Press studs	200	0.06	12
Belts	100	0.1	10
Buttons	10	0.7	7
			39

39 hours × £8 per hour = £312

ABSORPTION AND MARGINAL COSTING

25   B

The marginal cost of a product is the additional cost of producing an extra unit and is therefore the sum of the variable costs. If the inventory increases over a year, absorption costing profit will be higher than marginal costing profit because an element of fixed cost will be carried forward in closing inventory to be charged against profit in a future period.

26   A

Total contribution will increase as sales volume increases, but the contribution per unit will be constant as long as the sales price and variable cost per unit are unchanged. Overhead is not absorbed into the product unit so there is no under/over absorption of overhead. Marginal costing *does* provide useful information for decision making because it highlights contribution, which is a relevant cash flow for decision-making purposes.

27   The cost per mile under:

(a)   Marginal costing

Fuel and other variable overheads	£ per mile
Total variable cost per mile £9,200 / 4,600 miles	**2.00**

(b)   Absorption costing

Fuel and other variable overheads	£ per mile
Total variable cost per mile £9,200 / 4,600 miles	2.00
Drivers' wages, pension and national insurance £3,220 / 4,600 miles	0.70
Fixed overheads £23,000 / 4,600 miles	5.00
Total absorption cost per mile	**7.70**

28

Marginal Costing

	£000	£000
Sales		50,000
Opening inventory	0	
Production costs (7,560 + 17,640)	25,200	
Closing inventory (25,200/1,800 × 800)	−11,200	
Cost of sales		−14,000
Contribution		36,000
Fixed costs (3,600+2010)		−5,610
Profit for the period		30,390

Absorption Costing

	£000	£000
Sales		50,000
Opening inventory	0	
Production costs (7,560 + 17,640 + 3,600)	28,800	
Closing inventory (28,800/1,800 × 800)	−12,800	
Cost of sales		−16,000
Gross Profit		34,000
Non-production cost		−2,010
Profit for the period		31,990

Reconcile the two profits:

Absorption costing profit	31,990
Change in inventory × OAR (0–200) × (3,600/1,800)	−1,600
Marginal costing profit	30,390

29

Marginal Costing

	£	£
Sales (12 × 12,000)		144,000
Opening inventory (7 × 2,000)	14,000	
Production costs (7 × 15,000)	105,000	
Closing inventory (7 × 5,000)	−35,000	
Cost of sales		−84,000
Contribution		60,000
Fixed costs		−30,000
Profit for the period		30,000

Absorption Costing

	£	£
Sales (12 × 12,000)		144,000
Opening inventory (9 × 2,000)	18,000	
Production costs (9 × 15,000)	135,000	
Closing inventory (9 × 5,000)	−45,000	
Cost of sales		−108,000
Gross Profit		36,000
Non-production cost		0
Profit for the period		36,000

Reconcile the two profits:

Absorption costing profit	36,000
Change in inventory × OAR (2,000–5,000) × (30,000/15,000)	−6,000
Marginal costing profit	30,000

30 (a)

	£
Selling price/unit	40
Prime cost/unit	(12)
Variable production cost/unit	(4)
Contribution/unit	24

(b)

	£
Selling price/unit	40
Marginal cost/unit	(16)
Fixed production cost/unit	(10)
(£120,000/12,000 units)	
Profit/unit	14

(c)

Marginal Costing

	£	£
Sales (40 × 10,000)		400,000
Opening inventory (16 × 500)	8,000	
Production costs (16 × 12,000)	192,000	
Closing inventory (16 × 2,500)	-40,000	
Cost of sales (check: 10,000 × 16)		-160,000
Contribution (check: 10,000 × 24)		240,000
Fixed costs		-120,000
Profit for the period		120,000

Absorption Costing

	£	£
Sales (40 × 10,000)		400,000
Opening inventory (26 × 500)	13,000	
Production costs (26 × 12,000)	312,000	
Closing inventory (26 × 2,500)	-65,000	
Cost of sales		-260,000
Profit for the period		140,000

31 B

In an absorption costing system, the fixed cost per unit would be £3,000/15,000 units = £0.20 per unit.

By switching to absorption costing, in a period when inventory levels increase by 2,000 units, absorption costing profit would be higher by 2,000 units × fixed cost per unit, i.e. by 2,000 × £0.20 = £400.

Absorption costing profit = £23,000 + £400 = £23,400.

ACCOUNTING FOR OVERHEADS

OVERHEAD ALLOCATION AND APPORTIONMENT

32 D

Cost apportionment is concerned with sharing costs according to benefit received.

33

	Basis of apportionment	Wood cutting £	Wood finishing £	Maintenance £	Stores £	General Admin £	Totals £
Depreciation of plant and equipment	NBV of plant and equipment	1,013,229	434,241	-	-	-	1,447,470
Power for production machinery	Production machinery power usage (KwH)	772,200	514,800	-	-	-	1,287,000
Rent and rates	Floor space	-	-	94,050	56,430	37,620	188,100
Light and heat	Floor space	-	-	20,790	12,474	8,316	41,580
Indirect labour	Allocated	-	-	182,070	64,890	432,180	679,140
Totals		1,785,429	949,041	296,910	133,794	478,116	3,643,290
Reapportion Maintenance		207,837	89,073	(296,910)			
Reapportion Stores		86,966	46,828		(133,794)		
Reapportion General Admin		239,058	239,058			(478,116)	
Total overheads to production centres		2,319,290	1,324,000				3,643,290

34

	Basis of apportionment	Assembly £	Finishing £	Maintenance £	Stores £	General Admin £	Totals £
Depreciation of plant and equipment	NBV of plant and equipment	420,000	280,000	-	-	-	700,000
Power for production machinery	Production machinery power usage (KwH)	403,000	217,000	-	-	-	620,000
Rent and rates	Floor space	-	-	48,000	32,000	20,000	100,000
Light and heat	Floor space	-	-	9,600	6,400	4,000	20,000
Indirect labour	Allocated	-	-	102,000	40,000	240,000	382,000
Totals		823,000	497,000	159,600	78,400	264,000	1,822,000
Reapportion Maintenance		88,000	88,000	52,800	35,200	(264,000)	
Reapportion Stores		56,800	34,080	22,720	(113,600)		
Reapportion General Admin		176,340	58,780	(235,120)			
Total overheads to production centres		1,144,140	677,860				1,822,000

35

	Basis of apportionment	Scheduled services	Charter flights	Aircraft maintenance and repairs	Fuel and parts store	General Admin £	Totals £
		£000	£000	£000	£000	£000	£000
Depreciation of aircraft	NBV of aircraft	21,840	14,560	-	-	-	36,400
Aviation fuel and other variables	Planned number of miles flown	23,210	18,990	-	-	-	42,200
Pilots and aircrew salaries	Allocated	5,250	4,709	-	-	-	9,959
Rent and rates and other premises costs	Floor space	-	-	6,300	3,780	2,520	12,600
Indirect labour	Allocated	-	-	9,600	3,200	7,800	20,600
Totals		50,300	38,259	15,900	6,980	10,320	121,759
Reapportion Maintenance and repairs		9,540	6,360	(15,900)			
Reapportion fuel and parts store		3,839	3,141		(6,980)		
Reapportion General Admin		5,160	5,160			(10,320)	
Total overheads to profit centres		68,839	52,920				121,759

36

	Basis of apportionment	Plastics Moulding	Labelling	Stores	Equipment Maintenance	Totals
Heat and lighting fixed cost	Allocated	6,000	6,000	6,000	6,000	24,000
Heat and lighting variable cost	Square meters occupied	19,200	10,800	4,800	1,200	36,000
Power for machinery	Percentages	19,600	8,400	-	-	28,000
Supervision	Direct labour cost	50,000	70,000		-	120,000
Stores wages	Allocated	-	-	72,000	-	72,000
Equipment maintenance salaries	Allocated	-	-	-	188,200	188,200
Depreciation of non-current assets	NBV of non-current assets	48,000	24,000	9,000	3,000	84,000
Other overhead costs	Percentages	76,800	25,600	12,800	12,800	128,000
Totals		219,600	144,800	104,600	211,200	680,200
Reapportion Maintenance		70,400	70,400	70,400	(211,200)	
Reapportion Stores		130,200	44,800	(175,000)		
Total overheads to profit centres		420,200	260,000			680,200

OVERHEAD ABSORPTION

37 C

An absorption rate is used to determine the full cost of a product or service. Answer A describes overhead allocation and apportionment. Absorption does not control overheads, so answer D is not correct.

38 (a) OAR = 586,792/9,464 = £62

The correct answer is A

(b) Absorbed = 62 × 9,745 = £604,190

The correct answer is C

(c) Over absorption = 604,190 − 568,631 = £35,559 over absorbed

 The correct answer is A

39 (a) Assembly = 155,000/2,000 = £77.50 and Finishing = 105,000/1,750 = £60

The correct answer is B

(b) Assembly = 155,000/12,500 = £12.40 and Finishing = 105,000/8,750 = £12

The correct answer is D

(c) Assembly = 155,000 − 132,000 = £23,000 over absorbed and Finishing = 105,000 − 119,000 = £14,000 under absorbed

The correct answer is B

40 (a) Moulding = 36,000/18,000 = £2 and Painting = 39,000/13,000 = £3

The correct answer is D

(b) Moulding = £2 × 17,500 = £35,000 and Painting = £3 × 13,500 = £40,500

The correct answer is A

(c) Moulding = 35,000 − 37,500 = £2,500 under absorbed and Painting = 40,500 − 40,000 = 500 over absorbed.

The correct answer is B

41 (a) Mixing = 64,800/10,000 = £6.48 and Bagging = 70,200/2,340 = £30.00

The correct answer is A

(b) Mixing = £6.48 × 9,000 = £58,320 and Bagging = £30.00 × 2,120 = £63,600

The correct answer is C

(c) Mixing = 58,320 − 67,500 = £9,180 under absorbed and Bagging = 63,600 − 75,600 = £12,000 under absorbed.

The correct answer is B

42 A

Under- or over-absorption is determined by comparing the actual overhead expenditure with the overhead absorbed.

43 D

Fixed production overheads are over-absorbed when actual expenditure is less than budget and/or actual production volume is higher than budget.

44   D

Over-absorbed overheads increase profit, and so are recorded as a credit entry in either an over-absorbed overhead account or directly as a credit in the income statement. The matching debit entry could be either in the WIP account or the production overhead control account, depending on the costing system used.

45   C

Indirect labour is a costing concept. The double entry is:

Wages control		Overhead control	
	Indirect labour × (overheads)	Indirect labour × (wages)	

PROCESS COSTING

LOSSES

46

Description	Kg's	Unit cost £	Total cost £	Description	Kg's	Unit cost £	Total cost £
Material TR10	1,080	2.16	2,333	Normal loss	126	1.08	136
Material DG41	720	2.70	1,944	Output	2,300	8.316	19,127
Material IG11	720	1.10	792	Abnormal loss	94	8.316	782
Labour			5,760				
Overheads			9,216				
	2,520		20,045		2,520		20,045

47   D

Abnormal loss units are valued as one equivalent unit of cost, the same as units of good production. This cost is credited to the process account and debited to the abnormal loss account. The scrap value of abnormal loss is then credited to the abnormal loss account (with the matching debit to bank).

48 (a)

Description	Kg's	Unit cost £	Total cost £	Description	Kg's	Unit cost £	Total cost £
Material XG4	700	1.3	910	Normal loss	34	0.50	17
Material XH3	500	1.12	560	Output	1,600	4.93	7,888
Material XJ9	500	0.72	360	Abnormal loss	66	4.93	325
Labour			2,560				
Overheads			3,840				
	1,700		8,230		1,700		8,230

(b)

	Debit	Credit
Abnormal loss		✓
Abnormal gain	✓	

49

Description	Units	Unit cost £	Total cost £	Description	Units	Unit cost £	Total cost £
Input – Statues	300	11.25	3,375	Normal loss	30	5.00	150
Materials – Glaze			500	Output	290	49.35	14,312
Labour			5,760				
Overheads			3,840				
Abnormal gain	20	49.35	987				
	320		14,462		320		14,462

50 (a)

$$\frac{(500 \times 17.20) + (280 \times 10.50) + (86 \times 32) - (500 \times 5\% \times 1.68)}{500 - (500 \times 5\%)} = £30$$

(b)

Description	Litres	Cost per litre £	Total cost £		Description	Litres	Cost per litre £	Total cost £
Materials	500	17.20	8,600		Output	515	30.00	15,450
Labour			2,940		Normal loss	25	1.68	42
Overheads			2,752					
Abnormal gain	40	30.00	1,200					
	540		15,492			540		15,492

Note: do not be put off by the fact that more came out of the process than went in! Make sure you simply use the figures given. In real life the abnormal gain would be investigated to see why it had occurred (e.g. measurement error).

(b)

	Debit	Credit
Abnormal loss		✓
Abnormal gain	✓	

EQUIVALENT UNITS

51 **STATEMENT OF EU**

	Materials	Conversion
Completed	5,000	5,000
CWIP	600	300
TOTAL EU	5,600	5,300
Costs		
Period Costs	56,000	26,500
		10,600
TOTAL COSTS	56,000	37,100
Cost per EU	10.00	7.00

Valuation of Completed Output	£85,000
Valuation of CWIP	£8,100

Workings:

Completed = 5,000 × (£10 + £7) = £85,000

CWIP = 600 × £10 = £6,000

= 300 × £7 = £2,100

TOTAL = £8,100

52 C

Statement of EU

	Materials	Conversion
Completed	9,000	9,000
CWIP	3,500	2,625
TOTAL EU	12,500	11,625
Costs		
Period Costs	18,750	12,415
		16,415
TOTAL COSTS	18,750	28,830
Cost per EU	1.50	2.48

Valuation of Completed Output   £35,820

Workings:

Completed = 9,000 × (£1.50 + £2.48) = £35,820

53 B

Statement of EU

	Labour
Completed (7,000 × 100%)	7,000
CWIP (1,200 × 50%)	600
TOTAL EU	7,600
Costs	
Period Costs	3,800
TOTAL COSTS	3,800
Cost per EU	0.50

54 **Statement of EU**

Note: Using FIFO so the EU calculation focuses on costs incurred and work done this period.

	Materials	Conversion
OWIP to complete	0	100
Completed output	2,950	2,950
TOTAL EU	2,950	3,050
Costs		
Period Costs	123,900	91,500
TOTAL COSTS	123,900	91,500
Cost per EU	42	30

55 **C**

Note: Using FIFO so the EU calculation focuses on costs incurred and work done this period.

Equivalent units		Material	Conversion
	OWIP to complete	0	160
	Completed Output	400	400
	Total EU	400	560
Costs			
	Period	212	448
	Total cost	212	448
Cost per EU		0.53	0.80

56

Note: Using AVCO so the EU calculation will include all costs (including those b/f in OWIP) and all output, not just the work done this period.

Equivalent units		Material	Conversion
	Completed Output	3,200	3,200
	Total EU	3,200	3,200
Costs			
	OWIP	53,800	42,000
	Period	135,000	98,800
	Total cost	188,800	140,800
Cost per EU		59	44

57   D

Note: Using AVCO so the EU calculation will include all costs (including those b/f in OWIP) and all output, not just the work done this period.

Equivalent units		Material	Conversion
	Completed Output	9,000	9,000
	Total EU	9,000	9,000
	OWIP	400	150
	Period	950	750
	Total cost	1,350	900
Cost per EU		0.15	0.10

BASIC VARIANCE ANALYSIS

58   D

59

	Flexed Budget	Actual	Variance	Favourable F or Adverse A
Volume sold	267,000	267,000		
	£000	£000	£000	
Sales revenue	2,136	2,409	273	F
Less costs:				
Direct materials	534	801	267	A
Direct labour	267	267	0	0
Overheads	600	750	150	A
Operating profit	735	591	144	A

60

	Flexed Budget	Actual	Variance	Favourable F or Adverse A
Volume sold	28,800	28800		
	£000	£000	£000	
Sales revenue	4,320	3,877	443	A
Less costs:				
Direct materials	252	212	40	F
Direct labour	1,260	912	348	F
Overheads	445	448	3	A
Operating profit	2,363	2,305	58	A

61

	Flexed Budget	Actual	Variance	Favourable F or Adverse A
Volume sold	5,000	5,000		
	£000	£000	£000	
Sales revenue	1,875	1,950	75	F
Less costs:				
Direct materials	45	45	0	0
Direct labour	220	182	38	F
Overheads	89	90	1	A
Operating profit	1,521	1,633	112	F

SHORT TERM DECISION MAKING

COST VOLUME PROFIT ANALYSIS

62

(a) $\dfrac{64,800}{41.40 - 27} = 4,500 \text{ units}$

(b) $\dfrac{64,800}{14.4/41.4} = £186,300$

Or 4,500 × 41.4 = £186,300

(c)

Units of MR 13 sold	9,000	10,800
Margin of safety (units)	9,000 – 4,500 = 4,500 units	10,800 – 4,500 = 6,300 units
Margin of safety percentage	$\dfrac{9,000 - 4,500}{9,000} \times 100 = 50\%$	$\dfrac{10,800 - 4,500}{10,800} \times 100 = 58.33\%$

(d) $\dfrac{64,800 + 36,000}{14.4} = 7,000 \text{ units}$

(e) The correct answer is A – an increase in selling price means that contribution per unit increases therefore less units have to be made to cover the fixed costs. If BEP is lower then the margin of safety is higher.

63

(a) $\dfrac{£312,500}{£0.50/£0.80} = £500,000$

(b) $\dfrac{£312,500 + £200,000}{£0.50/£0.80} = £820,000$

(c) (i) £875,000 – £500,000 = £375,000

(ii) £375,000/£500,000 × 100 = 75%

64

(a)

	A (£)	B (£)	Total (£)
Selling price per unit	1.50	1.20	
Less: variable costs per unit			
Direct materials	0.20	0.25	
Direct labour	0.12	0.14	
Variable overheads	0.15	0.19	
Contribution per unit	1.03	0.62	
Sales volume (units)	300,000	500,000	
Total contribution	309,000	310,000	619,000
Less: fixed costs			264,020
Budgeted profit or loss			354,980

(b)

Product	A	B
Fixed costs (£)	158,620	105,400
Unit contribution (£)	1.03	0.62
Break-even sales (units)	154,000	170,000
Forecast sales (units)	250,000	400,000
Margin of safety (units)	96,000	230,000
Margin of safety (%)	38.40	57.50

(c)

Product A		Product B	✓

65

(a)

Likely miles	10,000	12,000	14,000
	£	£	£
Sales revenue	100,000	120,000	140,000
Variable costs:			
• Fuel	8,000	9,600	11,200
• Drivers' wages and associated costs	5,000	6,000	7,000
• Overheads	6,000	7,200	8,400
Fixed costs:			
• Indirect labour	10,600	10,600	10,600
• Overheads	25,850	25,850	25,850
Total cost	55,450	59,250	63,050
Total profit	44,550	60,750	76,950
Profit per mile	4.455	5.063	5.496

(b)

Forecast number of miles		12,000	14,000
Sales revenue	£	120,000	140,000
Fixed costs	£	36,450	
Contribution	£	97,200	
Contribution per mile	£	8.10	
Break-even number of miles	Miles	4,500	
Break-even sales revenue	£	45,000	
Margin of safety in number of miles	Miles	7,500	9,500
Margin of safety in sales revenue	£	75,000	95,000
Margin of safety	%	62.50	67.90

66

Line A is total revenue

Line B is total costs

Line C is total variable costs

Line D is fixed costs

LIMITING FACTOR ANALYSIS

67   D

Material required to meet maximum demand:

(6,000 × 3.25) + (8,000 × 4.75) =	57,500 litres
Material available:	50,000 litres

∴ Material is a limiting factor

Labour required to meet maximum demand:

(6,000 × 5) + (8,000 × 4) =	62,000 hours
Labour available:	60,000 hours

∴ Labour is a limiting factor

68

(a)

	Apple (£)	Banana (£)	Total (£)
Selling price per bar	3.00	2.40	
Less: variable costs per unit			
Direct materials	0.40	0.50	
Direct labour	0.24	0.28	
Variable overheads	0.30	0.38	
Contribution per unit	2.06	1.24	
Sales volume (bars)	75,000	125,000	
Total contribution	154,500	155,000	309,500
Less: fixed costs			150,000
Budgeted profit or loss			159,500

(b)

Product	Apple bars	Banana bars	Total
Contribution/unit (£)	2.06	1.24	
Machine hours/unit	0.40	0.16	
Contribution/machine hour (£)	5.15	7.75	
Product ranking	2	1	
Machine hours available			35,000
Machine hours allocated to: Product Banana Product Apple	15,000	20,000	
Units made	37,500	125,000	
Total contribution	77,250	155,000	232,250
Less: fixed costs (£)			150,000
Profit/loss made (£)			82,250

69

(a)

	Squeaker (£)	Hooter (£)	Total (£)
Selling price per unit	1.25	1.75	
Less: variable costs per unit			
Direct materials	0.50	0.25	
Direct labour	0.25	0.50	
Variable overheads	0.25	0.65	
Contribution per unit	0.25	0.35	
Sales volume (units)	80,000	70,000	
Total contribution	20,000	24,500	44,500
Less: fixed costs			15,000
Budgeted profit			29,500

(b)

Product	Squeaker	Hooter	Total
Contribution/unit (£)	0.25	0.35	
Machine hours/unit	0.50	0.25	
Contribution/machine hour (£)	0.50	1.40	
Product ranking	2	1	
Machine hours available			50,000
Machine hours allocated to: Product Hooter Product Squeaker	32,500	17,500	
Units made	65,000	70,000	
Total contribution	16,250	24,500	40,750
Less: fixed costs (£)			15,000
Profit made (£)			25,750

70

Product	AB1	CD2	EF3	Total
Contribution/pack (£)	4.00	5.00	3.00	
Kgs of plant extract/pack	0.40	0.25	0.50	
Contribution/kg (£)	10	20	6	
Product ranking	2	1	3	
Kgs of plant extract available				6,000
Kgs allocated to each product	2,640	1,730	1,630	
Number of packs to produce	6,600	6,920	3,260	
Total contribution earned (£)	26,400	34,600	9,780	70,780
Less: Fixed costs (£)				30,780
Profit/loss made (£)				40,000

71

(a)

	Asparagus soup	Broccoli soup	
	p	p	
Selling price per can	60	50	
Less: variable costs per can			
Direct materials	7	6	
Direct labour	6	7	
Variable overheads	2	3	
Contribution per can	45	34	
	No of cans	No of cans	
Sales volume (cans)	1,200,000	1,800,000	
	£	£	Total (£)
Total contribution	540,000	612,000	1,152,000
Less: fixed costs			652,000
Budgeted profit or loss			500,000

(b)

Product	Asparagus soup	Broccoli soup	Total
Contribution/can (£)	0.45	0.34	
Machine hours/can	0.005	0.005	
Contribution/machine hour (£)	90	68	
Product ranking	1	2	
Machine hours available			12,000
Machine hours allocated to: Product Asparagus Soup Product Broccoli Soup	6,000	6,000	
Units made	1,200,000	1,200,000	
Total contribution	540,000	408,000	948,000
Less: fixed costs (£)			652,000
Profit/loss made (£)			296,000

LONG TERM DECISION MAKING

NPV AND PAYBACK

72 (a)

	Year 0 £000	Year 1 £000	Year 2 £000	Year 3 £000
Capital expenditure	−1,620			
Sales income		756	1,008	1,440
Operating costs		−216	−270	−342
Net cash flows	−1,620	540	738	1,098
PV factors	1.0000	0.8696	0.7561	0.6575
Discounted cash flows	−1,620	470	558	722
Net present value	130			

The net present value is **positive**

(b)

Year	Cash flow £000	Cumulative cash flow £000
0	(1,620)	(1,620)
1	540	(1,080)
2	738	(342)
3	1,098	756

The payback period is **2** years and **4** months.

Months = 342/1,098 × 12 = 3.7 months

73 (a)

	Year 0 £000	Year 1 £000	Year 2 £000	Year 3 £000
Capital expenditure	−1,200			
Sales income		530	570	710
Operating costs		−140	−160	−170
Net cash flows	−1,200	390	410	540
PV factors	1.0000	0.8696	0.7561	0.6575
Discounted cash flows	−1,200	339	310	355
Net present value	−196			

The net present value is **negative**

(b)

Year	Cash flow £000	Cumulative cash flow £000
0	(1,200)	(1,200)
1	390	(810)
2	410	(400)
3	540	140

The payback period is **2** years and **9** months.

Months = 400/540 × 12 = 8.9 months

74 (a)

	Year 0 £000	Year 1 £000	Year 2 £000	Year 3 £000
Capital expenditure	−500			
Sales income		280	330	370
Operating costs		−100	−120	−140
Net cash flows	−500	180	210	230
PV factors	1.0000	0.909	0.826	0.751
Discounted cash flows	−500	164	173	173
Net present value	10			

The net present value is **positive**

(b)

Year	Cash flow £000	Cumulative cash flow £000
0	(500)	(500)
1	180	(320)
2	210	(110)
3	230	120

The payback period is **2** years and **6** months.

Months = 110/230 × 12 = 5.7 months

75

Machine A

	Year 0 £000	Year 1 £000	Year 2 £000	Year 3 £000
Capital expenditure	−1,085			
Operating costs		−200	−200	−200
Net cash flows	−1,085	−200	−200	−200
PV factors	1.0000	0.8696	0.7561	0.6575
Discounted cash flows	−1,085	−174	−151	−132
Net present cost	−1,542			

Machine B

	Year 0 £000	Year 1 £000	Year 2 £000	Year 3 £000
Capital expenditure	−1,200			
Operating costs		−150	−160	−170
Net cash flows	−1,200	−150	−160	−170
PV factors	1.0000	0.8696	0.7561	0.6575
Discounted cash flows	−1,200	−130	−121	−112
Net present cost	−1,563			

Bartrum should invest in **Machine A**

76

Van type P

	Year 0 £000	Year 1 £000	Year 2 £000	Year 3 £000
Capital expenditure	-600			
Disposal				150
Operating costs		-275	-290	-315
Net cash flows	-600	-275	-290	-165
PV factors	1.0000	0.8621	0.7432	0.6407
Discounted cash flows	-600	-237	-216	-106
Net present cost	-1,159			

Van type R

	Year 0 £000	Year 1 £000	Year 2 £000	Year 3 £000
Capital expenditure/disposal	-750			170
Operating costs		-345	-365	-390
Net cash flows	-750	-345	-365	-220
PV factors	1.0000	0.8621	0.7432	0.6407
Discounted cash flows	-750	-297	-271	-141
Net present cost	-1,459			

CPL should invest in **Van type P**

77 (a) No

(b) Yes

(c)

£	Nil

78

REPORT
To: The Chief Accountant
From: AAT student
Subject: Investment appraisal
Date: 3 December 20X2
The payback period of 2.4 years is *within* the company's policy of 3 years, and on this criterion the investment *should go* ahead.
The NPV is *negative** and on this criterion the investment *should not go* ahead.
The IRR, at 14%, is *below* the company's 16% cost of capital and on this criterion the investment *should not go* ahead.
Overall the investment *should not* proceed because the *NPV* is the dominant criterion.

Section 3

MOCK QUESTIONS

SECTION 1

TASK 1.1

The following information is available for superfine oil S07:

- Annual demand 78,125 litres.
- Annual holding cost per litre £2
- Fixed ordering cost £5

(a)   Calculate the Economic Order Quantity (EOQ) for S07

The inventory record shown below for superfine oil S07 for the month of July has not been completed for the month.

(b)   Complete the entries in the inventory record for the two receipts on 5 and 16 July that were ordered using the EOQ method. (Show the costs per litre (ltr) in £'s to 3 decimal places; and the total costs to the nearest £ – round down if 50p)

(c)   Complete ALL entries in the inventory record for the two issues in the month and for the closing balance at the end of July using the AVCO method of issuing inventory. (Show the costs per litre (ltr) in £'s to 3 decimal places; and the total costs to the nearest £ – round down if 50p)

Inventory record for superfine oil S07

Date	Receipts			Issues			Balance	
	Quantity Ltrs	Cost per Ltr (£)	Total cost (£)	Quantity Ltrs	Cost per Ltr (£)	Total cost (£)	Quantity Ltrs	Total cost (£)
Balance as at 1 July							210	420
5 July		2.10						
10 July				600				
16 July		2.20						
21 July				700				

TASK 1.2

Put the correct entries into the Journal below to record the following FOUR accounting transactions:

1   Receipt of oil into inventory paying by cheque.

2   Issue of oil from inventory to production.

3   Receipt of oil into inventory paying on credit.

4   Return of oil from inventory to supplier who had sold oil on credit.

The choices are:

A   Dr. Bank, Cr. Inventory

B   Dr. Trade Payables' Control, Cr. Inventory

C   Dr. Inventory, Cr. Bank

D   Dr. Inventory, Cr. Trade Payables' Control

E   Dr. Inventory, Cr. Production

F   Dr. Production, Cr. Inventory

	Choice
Transaction 1	
Transaction 2	
Transaction 3	
Transaction 4	

TASK 1.3

Below is a weekly timesheet for one of Sarloue Ltd's employees, who is paid as follows:

- For a basic seven and a half hour shift every day from Monday to Friday – basic pay.

- For any overtime in excess of the basic seven and a half hours, on any day from Monday to Friday – the extra hours are paid at time-and-a-half (basic pay plus an overtime premium equal to half of basic pay).

- For any hours worked on Saturday or Sunday – paid at double time (basic pay plus an overtime premium equal to basic pay).

Complete the columns headed Basic pay, Overtime premium and Total pay:

(Notes: Zero figures should be entered in cells where appropriate).

Employee's weekly timesheet for week ending 21 July

Employee: A. Lander			Profit Centre: Warehouse store man			
Employee number: S007			Basic pay per hour: £8.00			
	Hours spent in work	Hours spent on indirect work	Notes	Basic pay £	Overtime premium £	Total pay £
Monday	8	½	Late delivery			
Tuesday	7 ½					
Wednesday	8	½	Early delivery			
Thursday	8	½	Cleaning warehouse			
Friday	7 ½					
Saturday	4		Stock taking			
Sunday	2		Stock taking			
Total	**45**	**1 ½**				

TASK 1.4

Sarloue Ltd's budgeted overheads for the next financial year are:

	£000	£000
Depreciation of plant and equipment		22,250
Power for production machinery		17,500
Rent and rates		23,750
Light and heat		6,250
Indirect labour costs:		
Maintenance	10,000	
Stores	12,500	
Canteen	36,000	
Total indirect labour cost		58,500

The following information is also available:

Department	Net book value of plant and equipment	Production machinery power usage (KwH)	Floor space (square metres)	Number of employees
Production centres:				
Plastic moulding	180,000	22,500	2,000	20
Plastic extrusion	360,000	30,000	2,000	20
Support cost centres:				
Maintenance			1,000	2
Stores			3,000	2
Canteen			2,000	2
Total	540,000	52,500	10,000	24

Overheads are allocated or apportioned on the most appropriate basis. The total overheads of the support cost centres are then reapportioned to the two production centres using the direct method.

- 80% of the Maintenance cost centre's time is spent maintaining production machinery in the Plastic moulding production centre and the remainder in the Plastic extrusion production centre.
- The Stores cost centre supports the two production centres equally.
- The Canteen cost centre is reapportioned based on staff numbers.
- There is no reciprocal servicing between the three support cost centres.

Complete the overhead analysis table below:

	Basis of apportionment	Plastic moulding £000	Plastic extrusion £000	Maintenance £000	Stores £000	Canteen £000	Totals £000
Depreciation of plant and equipment							
Power for production machinery							
Rent and rates							
Light and heat							
Indirect labour							
Totals							
Reapportion Maintenance							
Reapportion Stores							
Reapportion Canteen							
Total overheads to production centres							

TASK 1.5

Sarloue Ltd's budgeted overheads and activity levels are:

	Plastic moulding	Plastic extrusion
Budgeted overheads (£000)	22,500	24,750
Budgeted direct labour hours	5,000	5,200
Budgeted machine hours	15,000	20,000

(a) What would the budgeted overhead absorption rate for each department, if this were set based on being heavily automated, to the nearest penny?

    A   Plastic moulding £1.50/hour, Plastic extrusion £1.24/hour

    B   Plastic moulding £1.50/hour, Plastic extrusion £0.62/hour

    C   Plastic moulding £3/hour, Plastic extrusion £0.62/hour

    D   Plastic moulding £3/hour, Plastic extrusion £1.24/hour

(b) What would the budgeted overhead absorption rate for each department, if this were set based on being labour intensive, to the nearest penny?

    A   Plastic moulding £4.50/hour, Plastic extrusion £2.38/hour

    B   Plastic moulding £4.50/hour, Plastic extrusion £4.76/hour

    C   Plastic moulding £9/hour, Plastic extrusion £4.76/hour

    D   Plastic moulding £9/hour, Plastic extrusion £2.38/hour

Additional data

At the end of the quarter actual overheads incurred were found to be:

	Plastic moulding	Plastic extrusion
Actual overheads (£)	19,800	38,000

(c) Assuming that exactly the same amount of overheads was absorbed as budgeted, what would be the under or over absorptions in the quarter?

    A   Plastic moulding over absorbed £2,700, Plastic extrusion over absorbed £13,250

    B   Plastic moulding over absorbed £2,700, Plastic extrusion under absorbed £13,250

    C   Plastic moulding under absorbed £2,700, Plastic extrusion under absorbed £13,250

    D   Plastic moulding under absorbed £2,700, Plastic extrusion over absorbed £13,250

SECTION 2

TASK 2.1

Sarloue Ltd has prepared a forecast for the next quarter for one of its engineered components, GG57. The forecast is based on selling and producing 1,000,000 units.

One of the customers of Sarloue Ltd has indicated that it may be significantly increasing its order level for component GG57 for the next quarter and it appears that activity levels of 1,500,000 and 2,000,000 units are feasible.

The semi-variable costs should be calculated using the high-low method. If 2,000,000 units are sold the total semi-variable cost will be £60,000,000 and there is a constant unit variable cost up to this volume.

Complete the table below and calculate the estimated profit per batch of GG57 at the different activity levels.

Units produced and sold	1,000,000	1,500,000	2,000,000
	£000	£000	£000
Sales revenue	469,750		
Variable costs:			
• Direct materials	65,000		
• Direct labour	97,500		
• Overheads	78,500		
Semi-variable costs:	40,000		
• Variable element			
• Fixed element			
Total cost	281,000		
Total profit	188,750		
Profit per unit to 2 decimal places	£188.75		

TASK 2.2

Product GG99 has a selling price of £29 per unit with a total variable cost of £21 per unit. Sarloue Ltd estimates that the fixed costs per quarter associated with this product are £9,952.

(a) Calculate the budgeted breakeven, in units, for product GG99.

units

(b)   Calculate the budgeted breakeven, in revenue, for product GG99.

£ [   ]

(c)   Complete the table below to show the budgeted margin of safety in units and the margin of safety percentage if Sarloue Ltd sells 5,000 units or 6,000 units of product GG99.

Units of GG29 sold	5,000	6,000
Margin of safety (units)		
Margin of safety percentage to 2 decimal places		

(d)   If Sarloue Ltd wishes to make a profit of £48,000, how many units of GG99 must it sell?

[   ] units

(e)   If Sarloue Ltd decreases the selling price of GG99 by £1 what will be the impact on the breakeven point and the margin of safety assuming no change in the number of units sold?

A   The breakeven point will decrease and the margin of safety will increase

B   The breakeven point will stay the same but the margin of safety will decrease

C   The breakeven point will decrease and the margin of safety will stay the same

D   The breakeven point will increase and the margin of safety will decrease

TASK 2.3

The Plastic extrusion department of Sarloue Ltd uses process costing for some of its products.

The process account for January for one particular process has been partly completed but the following information is also relevant:

Two employees worked on this process during January. Each employee worked 37.5 hours per week for 4 weeks and was paid £8 per hour.

Overheads are absorbed on the basis of £12.50 per labour hour.

Sarloue Ltd expects a normal loss of 10% during this process, which it then sells for scrap at 60p per kg.

(a)   Complete the process account below for December.

Description	Kgs	Unit cost £	Total cost £		Description	Kgs	Unit cost £	Total cost £
Material A	250	6			Normal loss		0.60	
Material B	425	4			Output	675		
Material C	75	5						
Labour								
Overheads								
	750							

(b)   Identify the correct entry for each of the following in a process account.

	Debit	Credit
Abnormal loss		
Abnormal gain		

TASK 2.4

Sarloue Ltd has the following original budget and actual performance for product GG101 for the year ending 31 December.

	Budget	Actual
Volume sold	20,000	18,500
Sales revenue	40,000	38,850
Less costs:		
Direct materials	16,000	17,575
Direct labour	10,000	10,175
Overheads	2,000	1,950
Operating profit	12,000	9,150

Both direct materials and direct labour are variable costs, but the overheads are fixed.

Complete the table below to show a flexed budget and the resulting variances against this budget for the year. Show the actual variance amount, for sales and each cost, in the column headed 'Variance' and indicate whether this is Favourable or Adverse by entering F or A in the final column. If neither F nor A enter 0.

	Flexed Budget	Actual	Variance	Favourable F or Adverse A
Volume sold		18,500		
Sales revenue		38,850		
Less costs:				
Direct materials		17,575		
Direct labour		10,175		
Overheads		1,950		
Operating profit		9,150		

TASK 2.5

One of the extrusion machines in the Plastic extrusion department is nearing the end of its useful life and Sarloue Ltd is considering purchasing a replacement machine.

Estimates have been made for the initial capital cost, sales income and operating costs of the replacement machine, which is expected to have a useful life of three years:

	Year 0 £000	Year 1 £000	Year 2 £000	Year 3 £000
Capital expenditure	450			
Other cash flows:				
Sales income		600	650	750
Operating costs		420	480	510

The company appraises capital investment projects using a 15% cost of capital.

(a) Complete the table below and calculate the net present value of the proposed replacement machine (to the nearest £000).

	Year 0 £000	Year 1 £000	Year 2 £000	Year 3 £000
Capital expenditure				
Sales income				
Operating costs				
Net cash flows				
PV factors	1.0000	0.8696	0.7561	0.6575
Discounted cash flows				
Net present value				

The net present value is *positive/negative**

*delete as appropriate

(b) Calculate the payback of the proposed replacement machine to the nearest whole month.

The payback period is ---------- Year(s) and ------------ Months

Section 4

ANSWERS TO MOCK QUESTIONS

SECTION 1

TASK 1.1

(a)   The EOQ = $\sqrt{\frac{2 \times 5 \times 78,125}{2}} = 625$

(b)   Inventory record card

Date	Receipts			Issues			Balance	
	Quantity Ltrs	Cost per Ltr (£)	Total cost (£)	Quantity Ltrs	Cost per Ltr (£)	Total cost (£)	Quantity Ltrs	Total cost (£)
Balance as at 1 July							210	420
5 July	625	2.10	1,312				835	1,732
10 July				600	2.074	1,244	235	488
16 July	625	2.20	1,375				860	1,863
21 July				700	2.166	1,516	160	347

TASK 1.2

	Choice
Transaction 1	(C) Dr. Inventory, Cr. Bank
Transaction 2	(F) Dr. Production, Cr. Inventory
Transaction 3	(D) Dr. Inventory, Cr. Trade Payables control
Transaction 4	(B) Dr. Trade Payables control, Cr. Inventory

TASK 1.3

Employee's weekly timesheet for week ending 21 July

Employee: A. Lander			Profit Centre: Warehouse store man			
Employee number: S007			Basic pay per hour: £8.00			
	Hours spent in work		*Notes*	*Basic pay £*	*Overtime premium £*	*Total pay £*
Monday	8	½	Late delivery	64	2	66
Tuesday	7½			60	0	60
Wednesday	8	½	Early delivery	64	2	66
Thursday	8	½	Cleaning warehouse	64	2	66
Friday	7 ½			60	0	60
Saturday	4		Stock taking	32	32	64
Sunday*	2		Stock taking	16	16	32
Total	**37**	**1 ½**		360	54	414

* Alternative answer for Sunday

Sunday*	2		Stock taking	0	32	32
Total	**37**	**1 ½**		344	70	414

TASK 1.4

	Basis of apportionment	Plastic moulding £000	Plastic extrusion £000	Maintenance £000	Stores £000	Canteen £000	Totals £000
Depreciation of plant and equipment	NBV of plant and equipment	7,417	14,833				22,250
Power for production machinery	Production machinery power usage (KwH)	7,500	10,000				17,500
Rent and rates	Floor space	4,750	4,750	2,375	7,125	4,750	23,750
Light and heat	Floor space	1,250	1,250	625	1,875	1,250	6,250
Indirect labour	Allocated			10,000	12,500	36,000	58,500
Totals		20,917	30,833	13,000	21,500	42,000	128,250
Reapportion Maintenance		10,400	2,600	(13,000)			
Reapportion Stores		10,750	10,750		(21,500)		
Reapportion Canteen		21,000	21,000			(42,000)	
Total overheads to production centres		63,067	65,183				128,250

TASK 1.5

(a)   Plastic moulding = 22,500/15,000 = £1.50 and Plastic extrusion = 24,750/20,000 = £1.24.

The correct answer is A

(b)   Plastic moulding = 22,500/5,000 = £4.50 and Plastic extrusion = 24,750/5,200 = £4.76.

The correct answer is B

(c)   Plastic moulding = 22,500 – 19,800 = £2,700 over absorbed and Plastic extrusion = 24,750 – 38,000 = £13,250 under absorbed.

The correct answer is B

SECTION 2

TASK 2.1

Units produced and sold	1,000,000	1,500,000	2,000,000
	£000	£000	£000
Sales revenue	469,750	704,625	939,500
Variable costs:			
• Direct materials	65,000	97,500	130,000
• Direct labour	97,500	146,250	195,000
• Overheads	78,500	117,750	157,000
Semi-variable costs:	40,000		
• Variable element		30,000	40,000
• Fixed element		20,000	20,000
Total cost	281,000	411,500	542,000
Total profit	188,750	293,125	397,500
Profit per unit (£)	£188.75	£195.42	£198.75

TASK 2.2

(a) $\dfrac{9,952}{29-21} = 1,244$ units

(b) $\dfrac{9,952}{8/29} = £36,076$

Or $1,244 \times 29 = £36,076$

(c)

Units of GG99 sold	5,000	6,000
Margin of safety (units)	$5,000 - 1,244 = 3,756$ units	$6,000 - 1,244 = 4,756$
Margin of safety percentage	$\dfrac{5,000 - 1,244}{5,000} \times 100 = 75.12\%$	$\dfrac{6,000 - 1,244}{6,000} \times 100 = 79.27\%$

(d) $\dfrac{9,952 + 48,000}{8} = 7,244$ units

(e) The correct answer is D – a reduction in selling price means that contribution per unit reduces therefore more units have to be made to cover the fixed costs. If BEP is higher than the margin of safety is lower.

TASK 2.3

Description	Kg's	Unit cost £	Total cost £		Description	Kg's	Unit cost £	Total cost £
Material A	250	6	1,500		Normal loss	75	0.60	45
Material B	425	4	1,700		Output	675	14.34	9,680
Material C	75	5	375					
Labour			2,400					
Overheads			3,750					
	750		9,725			750		9,725

	Debit	Credit
Abnormal loss		✓
Abnormal gain	✓	

TASK 2.4

	Flexed Budget	Actual	Variance	Favourable F or Adverse A
Volume sold	18,500	18,500		
Sales revenue	37,000	38,850	1,850	F
Less costs:				
Direct materials	14,800	17,575	2,775	A
Direct labour	9,250	10,175	925	A
Overheads	2,000	1,950	50	F
Operating profit	10,950	9,150	1,800	A

TASK 2.5

(a)

	Year 0 £000	Year 1 £000	Year 2 £000	Year 3 £000
Capital expenditure	(450)			
Sales income		600	650	750
Operating costs		420	480	510
Net cash flows	(450)	180	170	240
PV factors	1.0000	0.8696	0.7561	0.6575
Discounted cash flows	(450)	157	129	158
Net present value	(6)			

The net present value is **negative**

(b)

Year	Cash flow £000	Cumulative cash flow £000
0	(450)	(450)
1	180	(270)
2	170	(100)
3	240	140

The payback period is **2** years and **5** months.

Months = 100/240 × 12 = 5 months